Cape Cod and the Islands
Where Beauty and History Meet

PAINTINGS & TEXT BY KATHRYN KLEEKAMP

Dedication

To my husband Charles and children,
Liz, Scott and Russ

"Strawberries" © Olga Lyubkina. Image from BigStockPhoto.com.
"Blueberries" © Rebecca Spiker. Image from BigStockPhoto.com.

Designed by John P. Cheek
Type set in Bweeti/GoudyOlSt BT

ISBN: 978-0-7643-3317-0
Printed in China

Schiffer Books are available at special discounts for bulk purchases for sales promotions or premiums. Special editions, including personalized covers, corporate imprints, and excerpts can be created in large quantities for special needs. For more information contact the publisher:

Published by Schiffer Publishing Ltd.
4880 Lower Valley Road
Atglen, PA 19310
Phone: (610) 593-1777; Fax: (610) 593-2002
E-mail: Info@schifferbooks.com

For the largest selection of fine reference books on this and related subjects, please visit our web site at www.schifferbooks.com
We are always looking for people to write books on new and related subjects. If you have an idea for a book please contact us at the above address.

This book may be purchased from the publisher.
Include $5.00 for shipping.
Please try your bookstore first.
You may write for a free catalog.

In Europe, Schiffer books are distributed by
Bushwood Books
6 Marksbury Ave.
Kew Gardens
Surrey TW9 4JF England
Phone: 44 (0) 20 8392 8585; Fax: 44 (0) 20 8392 9876
E-mail: info@bushwoodbooks.co.uk
Website: www.bushwoodbooks.co.uk

CONTENTS

ACKNOWLEDGMENTS

Many individuals need to know how much I appreciate their help contributing to the completion of this book. First, thank you to my husband and patient reader, Charles. I'm grateful for the time, gentle criticism, helpful suggestions, and constant support he provided. Mary Sicchio, Special Collections Librarian at the William Brewster Nickerson Cape Cod History Archives at Cape Cod Community College in Hyannis, not only found documents and photos I requested, but willingly searched for others in the scope of my quest. She worked diligently scanning and providing many digital images for this collection. Hope Morrill, curator at the Salt Pond Visitor Center in Eastham was indispensable, not only for her "sleuthing" to find old photos, but her persistence and enthusiasm furnishing information. Randy Hunt, with his superb attention to detail, helped proof read my entire manuscript.

Neighbor and friend, Jim Coogan deserves a large thank you. A Cape Cod author, respected for his knowledge and love of Cape Cod history, Jim generously gave me his time and made significant suggestions that improved my work. Another neighbor, Ben Merrill, who has a home on Martha's Vineyard, patiently drove me all over the island so I might take photos used for some of the paintings in this book. Ben and his lovely wife, Betty, were kind enough to offer helpful criticism after reviewing my chapter on the Vineyard. My daughter Liz, in the midst of moving, getting married and starting a new job, willingly provided graphic and design suggestions. Sons Scott and Russell provided honest feedback and suggestions on my questions ranging from cover design to recipes.

I would not have gotten past a book concept without the help and support of Christie Lowrance. A talented writer and instructor at Cape Cod Community College, Christie has been a source of guidance and encouragement from the very beginning. Others who helped direct me at the start were Vicky Uminowicz, manager of Titcomb's Bookshop in Sandwich and Cynthia Bushong, manager of the Salt Pond Visitor Center Bookstore in Eastham. Both helped me appreciate the need for a book combining art and history that many visitors to this area often request.

Lincoln Thurber, Department Head of the Reference Department in the Nantucket Atheneum was generous with his time and willingness allowing me access to books in their historic collection. Thanks also to Lucy Loomis, Director of the Sturgis Library in Barnstable for scanning and providing images. Marie Henke and Georgen Charnes in the Research Library of the Nantucket Historical Association could not have been more considerate furnishing images.

Maureen Rukstalis, Administrator of the Historical Society of Old Yarmouth, and Linda Wilson, Librarian, Martha's Vineyard Historical Museum both successfully fought computer foibles processing large file images and met my requests with a smile. Paula Peters, Associate Director of Marketing at Plimoth Plantation reviewed my draft material on the Wampanoag native tribe and granted permission to use photographs taken at the plantation. Without any hesitation, Carl Borchert of Nantucket reviewed my chapter on that "faraway" island. Karen Deady offered helpful ideas and recipe suggestions. Herb Holden, whom I consider my art mentor, needs to be recognized. In the absence of a formal education in art, my weekly group painting sessions with Herb and others for the past five years have been invaluable in my development as an artist.

Finally, a sincere thank you to Pete Schiffer and Douglas Congdon-Martin at Schiffer Publishing. You have made me feel like a family member making this endeavor most enjoyable.

INTRODUCTION

Cape Cod and its neighboring islands, Martha's Vineyard and Nantucket, provide beauty at every turn. The vision may be simple or extraordinary…from a lone dory on a Wellfleet beach, to a crimson sunset over Menemsha Bay, to a Nantucket street lamp on a foggy, rain-kissed day. Every season, every hour transforms the landscape anew. This book is my attempt to pay homage to the splendor of the place that I call home.

Importantly, it's also about sharing some of the heritage that has made this area so unique and appealing to those who enjoy it. The essence of the Cape is far more than pristine beaches and windswept dunes. The Cape and Islands have a rich and unique heritage shaped by people who were hardworking, practical, courageous, and resourceful. Their stories deserve to be told and retold. Beyond the tales about daring shipmasters that sailed the world, there are stories of homemakers, lighthouse keepers, lifesavers, farmers and fishermen. All contributed to a legacy as rich and glorious as the land.

While Plymouth, Massachusetts is known for being the first settlement of the Pilgrims, it was Cape Cod's shore that greeted them at the end of their tortuous Atlantic journey in 1620. In fact, the Pilgrim Fathers considered moving the entire Plymouth settlement to what is today's town of Eastham on the outer Cape. Within two decades after Plymouth Colony was established, many of those "first comers," as they were known, returned to the Cape to build homes and farms. About that same time, early colonists were also settling Martha's Vineyard and Nantucket. These settlements spawned whaling, deep sea fishing, and salt making …industries that were essential to our nation's growth and prosperity. Arts and culture thrived as artists and writers sought splendid isolation and refuge from the constraints of city life. Now, more than ever, people come to this area, guided by a passion to live intimately with land and sea or perhaps just to savor a few glorious days to renew the spirit.

I first thought of compiling this book as I witnessed the interest of those who took the time to read the historical vignettes I put on the back of my art prints. I realized that I was giving them snippets, but they wanted more. This book is just that. It is a compilation of paintings and photographs, including many rare historic images, which provide a backdrop for the stories within. My biggest challenge has been to refine almost four hundred years of history into a modest volume; clearly, many other stories deserve to be told. In the bibliography I refer to many superb books that more fully elaborate the history of Cape Cod and the Islands. At the end of the book there is also a list of area historic associations, as well as art organizations. On these pages, I hope to convey the extraordinary beauty and compelling heritage of Cape Cod and the Islands.

Kathryn Kleekamp

Sandy Neck Beach, 2003, oil on canvas panel, 11 x 14.

CHAPTER ONE
THE CAPE COD LANDSCAPE

The breakers looked like droves of a thousand wild horses of Neptune,
rushing to the shore, with their white manes streaming far behind.
—Henry David Thoreau, *Cape Cod*

Beach

One August many years ago, when I was about twelve, my mother and I spent a week at a seaside cottage in New Jersey. I woke up early one morning, went out, and sat on the porch steps overlooking the beach. After gazing at the sea for a few minutes, I remember being overcome with a strange and somewhat frightening feeling of eternity. The vast ocean melting into an infinite sky, unceasing waves beating the shore, and the endless stretch of beach … all had stirred a sense of timelessness, a concept that my young mind could not yet understand. We lived in an apartment building on a busy street in uptown Manhattan. My normal world consisted of high-rise apartments, cement playgrounds, and noisy traffic. Some years later, I realized that visit to the beach was the first time I experienced the natural world in its purest form, and it was quite overwhelming.

A solitary walk on the beach is one of the most sensory rewarding ways to connect with nature. The warming rays of the sun, cool water bathing the toes, the taste of salt air, sounds of laughing gulls overhead … all envelop and restore. Every stroll is a journey of discovery and wonder: tiny sanderlings scurry together in concert like a filmy scarf hovering low over the sand. The perfect molt of a horseshoe crab lies half buried in the sand. A golden swarm of butterflies may pass overhead. Awareness of the fragility of our Cape Cod beaches enhances appreciation even more.

Once a solid bed of clay, this now sandy peninsula was formed by ancient passing glaciers and further molded by the wind and sea. Around 6,000 years ago, after the glaciers retreated, the melting water caused the sea level to rise. Attacking waves eroded the land, particularly during brutal winter storms, and created the cliffs we see on Cape Cod, Nantucket and Martha's Vineyard. The water reworked debris from the cliffs, producing sand and gravel, carrying it up and down the coast to form the beaches. This process is still very much ongoing. Vast amounts of sand are taken from the outer beaches of the Cape and redistributed onto coastal sandbars and north to the Provincetown hook. On Nantucket Island, the bluffs are eroding at a rate of three feet or more a year. No one can say for sure what Cape Cod will look like in the future, but we know it will change dramatically.

The Outermost House

Nature is a part of our humanity, and without some awareness and experience of that divine mystery man ceases to be man.
—Henry Beston, *The Outermost House: A Year of Life on the Great Beach of Cape Cod*

There have always been individuals who isolated themselves from the modern world and sought inspiration and restoration by living in a beach cottage. Cape Cod has produced many fine authors who have shared such an experience. Among these, two stand out. In 1926, writer and naturalist Henry Beston built a simple two-room dwelling on a cliff overlooking the outer beach in Eastham. He intended to spend a couple of weeks there but later wrote, "The fortnight ending, I lingered on, and as the year lengthened into autumn, the beauty and mystery of this earth and outer sea so possessed and held me that I could not go." Beston considered himself a "writer/naturalist" and is thought to be one of the fathers of the modern environmental movement. His book, *The Outermost House: A Year of Life on the Great Beach of Cape Cod*, was an inspirational force in the creation of the Cape Cod National Seashore. In his foreword to the eleventh printing of the book he wrote, "Bird migrations, the rising of the winter stars out of the breakers and the east, night and storm, the solitude of a January day, the glistening of dune grass in midsummer, all this is to be found between the covers even as today it is still to be seen." Driven by the relation of nature to the human spirit he tells us, "Nature is a part of our humanity, and without some awareness and experience of that divine mystery man ceases to be man."

Years later, after beach erosion forced its move, the Fo'c'sle (Beston's name for his cottage) was relocated inland. Nan Waldron Turner was another who was drawn to the natural world and spent the equal of a year there counting her visits over sixteen years beginning in 1961. She chronicled her experiences in *Journey to the Outermost House*. Nan's daughter, Les Waldron, shared her own recollections of staying in the house:

> Outermost wasn't just a cottage. It had a different purpose…a very different reason for being. It was a courageous little safe-harbor far along a spit of sand with no electricity or amenities save hand pump and gas lights. One chose to stay there (without cell phones) knowing there was not imminent rescue or neighbor to call. The house, and its guests endured, baked by the sun, plagued by insects, beaten by rain, ice, tides and pelting sand. It was the symbol of modest human presence slipped into the raw world of natural wonder…humbling to say the least.

Thankfully, both books endure. The Outermost House was washed out to sea in the great blizzard of 1978.

The Outermost House, 2006, oil on canvas panel, 9 x 12.

Sea

*The seas are the heart's blood of the earth. Plucked up and kneaded by
the sun and the moon, the tides are systole and diastole of earth's veins.
The rhythm of the waves beats in the sea like a pulse in living flesh. It
is pure force, forever embodying itself in a succession of watery shapes
which vanish on its passing.*
—Henry Beston, *The Outermost House: A Year of Life on the Great
Beach of Cape Cod*

Beaches may bring people to Cape Cod, but it's the vast sea, simultaneously splendid and terrifying, that impresses with its many moods and manifestations. On a clear day, the ocean can be refreshing and playful as we frolic in the surf. It can lull us to sleep as we float along in our cozy berth. But in the midst of a winter storm, the sea unleashes a terribly display of nature's most brutal and destructive forces.

The water also creates illusion. Although we think of ocean waves as water in motion, the water out beyond the surf zone, where waves break, hardly moves at all. A wave is formed by a pulse of energy transferred from the wind to the water. This energy flows beneath and through water that remains fairly motionless on the surface. You can see this yourself by watching a gull lazily floating out beyond the zone where the waves break. He will bob up and down but remain relatively stationary with each passing wave.

To understand this, imagine a clothesline stretched between two posts by a beach cottage. If you flick the line, it will undulate and form waves between its two poles. However, the fibers of the rope itself will not move back and forth, but merely up and down. Similarly, the ocean does not move. It's only when the front of the wave hits the shore and the back of the wave is still moving that the wave piles up on itself, cannot sustain its height and crests into a breaker that spills on the shore.

On the Cape and Islands the gravitational pull of the sun and moon, creates tidal patterns of two high tides and two low tides every day. This repetitive rhythm of tides sets the great diversity of behavior and creatures that inhabit the shoreline and marsh. Filter feeders such as clams, oysters and mussels feast on volumes of microscopic plankton washed up with the incoming tide. Fiddler crabs come out of their burrows to feed when the tide is out and go back into hiding when it returns, plugging their holes behind them. Marsh birds enjoy a delectable smorgasbord of fish served with each incoming rush of water.

Ocean's Edge, 2007, oil on canvas, 9 x 12.

Dunes

These hills, many of them so green that only the initiated realize that they are in reality sand dunes, with opening vistas through which one may catch a glimpse of the sea; with paths leading between them to the solitary and distant houses of which we may see only a bit of the roof.
—Agnes Edwards, *Cape Cod New and Old*

Standing in the vast secluded world of dune and sea on the Outer Cape, one is literally at land's end. This sandy tip of the Cape Cod peninsula lies farther out to sea than any other land mass on the east coast of the United States. The sand dunes here are one of nature's most beautiful phenomena. The vision of lofty sand forming undulating crests and contours under the backdrop of a blue sky or starlit night can be thrilling beyond description.

As we view the majestic dunes in today's Truro and Provincetown, it's difficult to imagine rich soil and dense forests once covered the land underneath. Describing how it looked to the Pilgrims as the *Mayflower* first touched shore, William Bradford wrote of a "whole countrie full of woods and thickets." The land was covered with "oaks, pines, juniper, sassafras and other sweet woods." A small remnant of these, a beech forest, can still be seen in Provincetown. Sadly, the early settlers decimated the trees. There were endless uses for wood: building homes and ships; burning it for warmth, fueling the fires of whaling and glassmaking industries. Fields were cleared for farms and woodlands were burned to release nutrients into the soil. Domestic use alone required about 40 cords of wood for an average family.

Over time, the ocean winds caused a massive shifting of sand onto the unprotected landscape. Sand dunes on young spits may be small, but the dunes on Monomoy Island and Provincetown reach heights up to 100 feet. Once formed, sand spits and dunes do not remain unchanged for long. The forces of wind and waves continue to transport and redeposit the sand. As early as the 1800s people realized the need to stabilize the dunes and they planted sea grass. These efforts increased in the 1960s when the Cape Cod National Seashore was created and the National Park Service began planting beach grass. Currently, the eroding cliffs lose one foot or more to the sea each year. It is felt that as the cliffs are consumed, the forces of the sea will disperse the delicate sands and ultimately claim the land.

Autumn Dunes, 2006, oil on canvas panel, 11 x 14.

Marsh

*To feel the breath of a mist moving over a great salt marsh, to watch the
flight of shore birds that have swept up and down the surf lines . . . to
see the running of the old eels and the young shad to the sea, is to have
knowledge of things that are as nearly eternal as any earthly life can be.*
—Rachel Carson, *Under the Sea Wind*

Beach and ocean may first come to mind when considering the Cape Cod landscape, but the salt marshes surrounding the ocean's countless tributaries are the areas of true mystery and wonder. Those who find time to visit the marsh will discover a Zen-like calmness as languorous grasses dotted with sea lavender gently sway in the breeze, ducks paddle lazily on an open patch of water, a lone osprey circles overhead. Beyond the visual beauty, it's the unique ability of marsh plants and animals to tolerate vast extremes in natural conditions that is truly impressive. No other habitat in nature is more dramatic or stressful. Flowing ocean tides bring fluctuations in salinity and variable water inundation. Summer temperatures on the marsh can vary over 50 degrees in a few hours when the cool water retreats and the sun bakes the earth.

A salt marsh is formed by the arrival of a seed of grass called *Spartina alterniflora*. The grass grows and spreads by means of a subterranean rhizome system. As roots are formed, they become dense and encourage the deposition of sediment and decayed material. This begins to create a terrestrial land mass and as other salt tolerant grasses invade, the area grows and meadows form. Between these meadows are creeks that have an extremely abundant and diverse population of plants and sea creatures. Mussels grow readily and can be quite densely packed. The byssal threads or silky filaments secreted by these mollusks bind the sediment and further enhance the growth of Spartina. Another common salt marsh resident, the fiddler crab, also aids in Spartina growth by burrowing and aerating the sediment.

Marsh estuaries are the spawning grounds and nursery areas for 75% of commercial and recreational fish species such as striped bass, bluefish and flounder. Untold thousands of other tiny fish-like mummichogs or sticklebacks who spend their lives in the marsh can be seen on closer observation. Hermit crabs scurry along the intertidal mudflats. Snails hold fast to their lodging at the base of the salty cord grass stems; sparrows and red-winged blackbirds nest in tidal marshes. Herons and snowy egrets visit the marsh attracted by the elaborate menu of seafood.

Evening Marsh, 2006, oil on canvas panel, 11 x 14.

Pond

But when its ice foundation finally melted, this land sank, forming pockets into which the ground water promptly seeped. These water pockets are today the ponds that are found scattered thickly over the whole length and breadth of the Cape.
—Henry C. Kittredge, Cape Cod: Its People and Their History

The morning is calm. Autumn's copper and bronze leaves reflect perfectly on the pond's mirror-like surface. A family of geese may paddle by, hardly an intrusion as their silent glide soothes the spirit. Here and there the gentle splash of leaping fish will cut the surface. A few fallen leaves drift along lazily. Unlike summer's crowded beaches, this tiny sea of tranquility seems one's own.

One of Cape Cod's best kept secrets is its almost 500 fresh water ponds. Although some are visible from main roads, most are hidden. They can be as large as the 743-acre Long Pond shared by Brewster and Harwich or as small as a garden plot. These ponds are a source of great fascination as scientists tell us that they were formed from huge blocks of ice that were deposited during the last ice age and over time melted, leaving deep depressions. These holes known as "kettles" remained dry for a long time as rainwater quickly percolated through the porous soil. As sea level increased, the freshwater table also rose and ultimately the ponds filled.

A number of these fresh water ponds became salt water ponds as the ocean encroached through inlets or breaks in barrier beaches. Ryder Cove in Chatham or Salt Pond in Eastham are examples. Fresh or salt water, each pond has its own distinct personality and inhabitants. It's heartening to know that even on the bleakest winter day resident swans and gulls find refuge on the pond surface while perch and bass continue feeding below.

Autumn Pond, 2005, oil on canvas panel, 8 x10.

Shawme Pond Swans

I have looked upon those brilliant creatures and
now my heart is sore...
—William Butler Yeats, *The Wild Swans at Coole*

I live on historic Shawme Pond in Cape Cod's oldest town, Sandwich. Many stories come to mind about the wildlife that frequent the pond and our nearby wetlands. I've rescued abandoned goslings, watched turtles slowly lumber up our lawn to lay eggs, and shared Thanksgiving dinner (cracked corn) with a visiting flock of wild turkeys. However, one particular story comes to mind and was my inspiration for the accompanying painting.

I delight in the annual event of watching the pond's resident pair of mute swans mate and build their nest while the air is still cool in early spring. The first sighting of newly hatched cygnets usually occurs, appropriately, around Mother's Day. Two years ago, according to their usual pattern, the swans had a beautiful family of eight cygnets. I was pleased when they made their appearance, right on schedule. Unfortunately, as we know, nature is not always kind. Our pond has many predators … snapping turtles, coyotes, raccoons, owls and so forth. One by one each of the offspring disappeared. Sadly, I watched the parents alone after bringing to life such a precious family.

Shortly after, however, I was surprised to see the pen (female) once again sitting on her nest. The nest was directly across the pond and I kept my field glasses at hand to watch her progress. This second nesting time seemed particularly long. I watched the pen, day after day, in rain and wind, patiently sitting on her nest …denying herself customary feedings and baths through the period. I was deeply touched at her unweary care. Weeks followed and she stayed fast on her nest. Finally, one day I saw the cob (male) and the pen in the water with six tiny forms at their side. My heart gladdened at the sight of a family once again. A week or so later, the pen and the cob came to our shore to visit. They were alone. I knew they would never leave their little ones behind and once again I was heartbroken over their loss. As they came closer, the pen opened her wings and I saw a beautiful cluster of tiny grey heads tucked in together on her back. Each one in turn, jumped off the mother's back and into the water. In an instant, my distress changed to joyous relief. Out of the six, five cygnets grew to adulthood. They were quite breathtaking to see as they flew overhead together, practicing for the journey that would take them to their own pond.

Shawme Pond Swans, 2003,
oil on canvas panel, 8 x 10.

The Mayflower II , launched in England in1956, is a replica of the 17th century *Mayflower*. Owned by Plimoth Plantation, it's moored with its two shallops in Plymouth Harbor, Plymouth MA.

BEGINNINGS

*Provincetown's generous harbor was so large that a thousand sail of
ships may safely ride…*
—Edward Winslow, *Mourt's Relation*

First Landing

More than most people realize, Cape Cod was a significant part of the early Pilgrim period. The month-long late fall sojourn of the Mayflower in Provincetown, while explorers scouted nearby areas, links it forever with 17th century New England history. On the 9th of November, 1620, after a difficult and storm-filled journey over the Atlantic, passengers on the Mayflower saw land. A narrative known as *Mourt's Relation*, compiled from firsthand accounts primarily by William Bradford and Edward Winslow, relates that, "by break of the day, we espied land, which we deemed to be Cape Cod, and so afterward it proved." Unable to navigate the hazardous coastal shoals and breakers and travel to their intended southern Virginia territory destination, they sailed northward around the tip of Cape Cod and dropped anchor on November 11th in what is today's Provincetown Harbor.

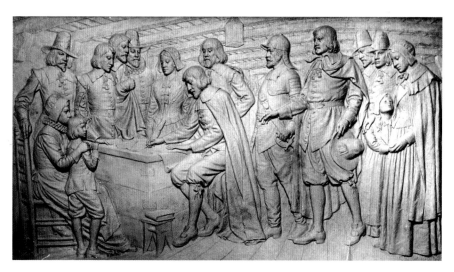

The Mayflower Compact was signed by all 41 of the adult males on board who consented to follow the regulations set forth. *Courtesy Nickerson Archives, Cape Cod Community College.*

One can only imagine the Pilgrims' relief and excitement after the long, tempestuous journey. Edward Winslow, in the same account, indicated the terrain revealed "oaks, pines, juniper, sassafras, and other sweet wood." Whales were abundant and he adds, "there was the greatest store of fowl that ever we saw." As eager as they were to explore the land, Winslow and Bradford recognized the need for a set of rules on conducting themselves. Bradford, in his *History of Plymouth Plantation, 1620-1647* wrote, there were "mutinous speeches" from some on board indicating, "when they came ashore they would use their own liberty, for none had power to command them." *The Mayflower Compact*, a social contract defining a set of fair and equal laws was drawn up. It is the first written document in American history that states majority opinion rules.

On the 15th of November a contingent of men, including William Bradford and Myles Standish, made their way inland by foot to find a suitable place for settlement. When they were about a mile inland, they saw five or six native Indians and a dog, who all quickly ran into the woods. In time they found a spring of fresh water. Having brought no beer or water to drink, they were extremely thirsty. In *Mourt's Relation*, Bradford writes, we "sat us down and drunk our first New England water, with as much delight as ever we drunk drink in all our lives." A short while later they came upon a hill where they unearthed an Indian cache of corn hidden in

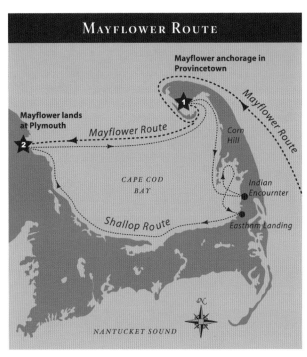

Route of the shallop that carried nineteen men led by Myles Standish. They explored the northwestern shores of Cape Cod before deciding upon Plymouth as a place to settle. *Map adapted from National Park Service Handbook by Liz Kleekamp.*

baskets. More valuable a find than gold, since they had no seed for the following year's crop, they dug it up to take back to the ship. Vowing to themselves to make restitution, they honored that pledge years later.

Although the area had a harbor, fertile land for growing corn and abundant fish, some of the first settlers were wary of building their permanent settlement there. The shallowness of the harbor would allow for only small boats and from previous explorations they knew of a more favorable harbor across the bay. They were also concerned that the only fresh water they found was in ponds which might dry up in the summer.

On December 6th, another expedition party went forth to explore further. They went by shallop, a small boat that could be rowed or sailed along the shore. The men traveled south along the northwestern coast of the Cape Cod peninsula looking for rivers and bays. The weather was numbingly cold, and they had to struggle to make progress against the freezing winds. William Bradford wrote, "for the water froze on our clothes, and made them many times like coats of iron." Finally, they made landfall near Nauset, known today as Eastham. Upon waking on December 8th and preparing for the day's journey onward, they were attacked by a small band of Indians. Several of the Pilgrims fired muskets, particularly at an Indian who was standing behind a nearby tree. He took off and yelled for others to follow him. Although arrows and gunshots were exchanged, there were no injuries on either side. First Encounter Beach in Eastham is named to commemorate that skirmish. Unnerved by the encounter and the fact that winter was fast approaching, it was urgent to find a permanent settlement.

The shallop continued along the coast heading for a place with a good harbor that John Coppin, their pilot, had remembered from a previous expedition. The weather turned fierce with high winds and a blinding snow storm. It was so severe, in fact, that the rudder broke, the mast snapped in three places and the sail fell overboard. Mustering what strength they had left, they rowed into Clark's Island at the mouth of Plymouth Harbor. After two days of rest and observing the Sabbath on Sunday, they departed on Monday morning and soon found what would be the ultimate destination they sought at Plymouth. They returned by shallop to Provincetown and sailed the Mayflower and its passengers to their permanent home where they finally dropped anchor for the last time in Plymouth Harbor on December 26, 1620. William Bradford later wrote in his journal, "That which was most sad and lamentable was that in two or three month's time half of the men on the shallop died." Many more, if not all of the passengers on the Mayflower, might have perished on Cape Cod, were it not for the fortitude and resilience of the sixteen men on the damaged vessel that would bring them to their new home.

Wampanoag Indians

Massasoit was the great sachem or leader of the Wampanoag Indians. He forged critical personal and political ties with the colonial leaders resulting in a negotiated peace treaty on March 22, 1621.

For thousands of years they did not alter the natural scene. They were part of it."
—Marie Fawsett, *Cape Cod Annals*

Twelve thousand years before European adventurers came to the area, Wampanoag Indians inhabited Cape Cod and the nearby islands. Their ancestors named this area "Land of the First Light." Although there are some accounts of skirmishes, a unique characteristic of the Wampanoags, unlike the more warlike Narragansett tribe, was their openness, albeit guarded, toward English explorers. When Bartholomew Gosnold anchored off the area between Monomoy and Eastham in 1602 he was met by canoes of non-threatening natives. Although there were several episodes of hostility that did occur, Henry Kittredge in, *Cape Cod, Its People and Their History*, explains them as "justified retaliation" for aggressive white men. In a letter back to England, Mayflower passenger, Edward Winslow, wrote,

> We have found the Indians very faithful in their covenant of peace with us, very loving, and ready to pleasure us. We, for our parts, walk as peaceably and safely the wood as in the highways in England. We entertain them familiarly in our houses and they as friendly bestowing their venison on us.

The affability of the natives, along with their hunting and farming skills, impressed the newcomers to write and encourage others in Europe to join them in this new land. The Indian Squanto was described by William Bradford as "a special instrument sent of God" for his willingness to show the Pilgrims how to fish, plant corn, and trade. A premonition of a darker side of what the native people would be subjected to is revealed in another passage in Winslow's letter: "They are a people without any religion or knowledge of any God, yet very trusty, quick of apprehension . . ." This apprehension seems justified, based on previous kidnappings of the natives by earlier European explorers in the 1500s. Interestingly, Squanto himself had been kidnapped in 1614 and sold into slavery in Spain. He managed to escape, travel to England, learn English, and make his way back to Cape Cod.

When the English colonists arrived at Plymouth (Pautuxet) on December 26th in 1620, the population of native Wampanoags was vastly diminished. War with the Narragansett tribe and pandemics of smallpox, spotted fever, and measles from exposure to early European fishermen had destroyed eighty percent of coastal tribes. In spite of diminished numbers, the Wampanoags could have easily destroyed the even more vulnerable English newcomers, half of whom perished from illness and exposure that first winter. Were it not for the woodlands the indigenous natives had already cleared producing open acreage, it's unlikely that there would have been any Mayflower survivors that following spring. In his book, *A Long Deep Furrow*, Howard S. Russell relates,

Those who think farming a simple operation little realize the vast differences in soils, climate and types of crops and animals; nor can they readily appreciate the importance of accumulated knowledge inherited locally from previous generations of husbandmen.

The arduous labor of clearing trees, digging roots, tilling the soil and fertilizing would have made any spring crop impossible for the early settlers, particularly since they brought no plows and would have to do the work by hand. In the warm weather native Wampanoags settled along the creeks and shores where marine foods were readily available. In the winter they moved inland to hunt deer and turkey. Summer homes near the water might be made of reeds, but winter dwellings were more substantial, with a cedar framework covered with layers of bark and maple exterior.

When the first white explorers arrived in the 1500s, New England native Indians were growing abundant crops of corn, squash, beans, pumpkins and tobacco. They were expert at fertilizing the fields with herring, and knew how to store crops in the earth to last through winter. Later, the English speaking native, Squanto, taught the English settlers these techniques and introduced them to the plants and animals of New England. The Wampanoags taught the colonists how to plant corn in small mounds with beans and squash planted around the stalks. The beans added nitrogen to replenish the soil. Unlike the later English leaders who protected crops by requiring early colonists to "shoot ten crows" per family, native Indians honored the crow for bringing the first corn seeds to them. They would always plant a few extra seeds in each mound for the crows who loved newly planted corn.

Reproduction of a Wampanoag "nushwetu" or "house of three fires" at Plimoth Plantation, Plymouth, Massachusetts. This recreation is an example of a dwelling for a three-generation family of 10-15 members.

Recreation of a native Wampanoag cornfield at Plimoth Plantation, Plymouth, Massachusetts. The platform in the center of the field was a place for children to play and women to work. The activity would keep animals away.

As thousands more European settlers came to Plymouth and other Massachusetts colonies, the soil became depleted by overuse and crop production diminished. Farmers also needed food for the increasing number of cattle. This set the stage for expansion. Cape Cod, close to the Aptucxet trading post, with abundant forests, open land, and vast salt marshes was an ideal choice. In the early 1600s, the Wampanoags on Cape Cod numbered about two thousand and were divided into a dozen sub-tribes including the Pamets, Nausets, Cummaquids, and Mattacheese. Their names are evident today on the Cape as names of ponds, beaches, and towns.

As English settlers made their way to the Cape from Plymouth, large parcels of land were seized or traded for token amounts. Wampanoag historians now cite the 1452 papal document known as the "Doctrine of Discovery" used by Spain, Portugal, England, and other Christian countries, which condoned the taking of land from non-Christians or from those perceived to worship pagan gods. Steve Newcomb in *Five Hundred Years of Injustice* writes, "Christian nations had a divine right, based on the Bible, to claim absolute title to and ultimate authority over any newly discovered non-Christian inhabitants and their lands." Another viewpoint is presented by historian R.A. Lovell Jr. in his book *Sandwich: A Cape Cod Town*. He writes, "...the Indians knew perfectly well what they were doing in selling these tracts." Adding, "A critical factor to them was protection from Indian rivals or enemies, rather than from the whites." The items traded, such as metal pots, knives, axes, were useful and also served as status symbols. As guns, horses and alcohol were traded, tribal life built on conservative traditions began to deteriorate. Sandwich resident, Richard Bourne was sympathetic to the plight of the natives. In 1658 he helped set aside 50 square miles in the town of Mashpee where the Indians could govern themselves with their own court of law. Today, the town, whose name came from the aboriginal Massippe,

meaning "Land of Great Cove," has the largest population of Wampanoags in Massachusetts. Although the tribe has evolved in many ways, they hold true to their ancestral customs and have a Tribal Council, Sachem (chief) and Medicine Man. They believe every aspect of the earth is sacred and alive. Animals, trees and man all have spirits and are part of a vast and complex web of life. The Mashpee Old Indian Meeting House, still used by the tribe for ceremonies, is the oldest Indian church in the United States. On the lower Cape the Wampanoags were largely destroyed. By 1764 there were only eleven natives in Wellfleet and four in Eastham. Today's Cape visitor may drive down well paved roads, but the Native Indian names of most of these roads remind us that this ancient land belonged to the Wampanoags.

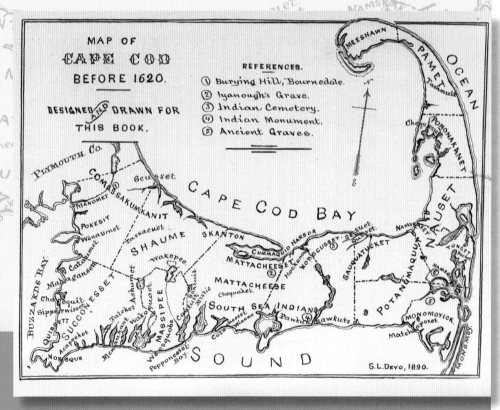

Map of Cape Cod Before 1620. Source: *History of Barnstable County, Massachusetts.* Simeon, Deyo, editor, 1890.

Establishing Trade

[The Aptucxet Trading Post] launched what is now the world's leading economic force: the American free enterprise system.
—Bourne Historical Society

We are familiar with the Pilgrims' struggle for survival that first winter in Plymouth: lack of food, exposure to cold and illness decimated half their small number. In addition, they were deeply in debt to the merchant adventurers who financed their voyage. According to George Lombard, in *Aptuxcet, a Trading Place of the Pilgrims*, the Plymouth Colony's debt "amounted to some twenty-four hundred pounds at an interest rate of at least thirty percent." To help the Pilgrims pay off their debt, William Bradford had the idea of establishing a trade route using the Manomet River flowing into Buzzards Bay from the south and Scusset Creek on the north. This inland trade route would also allow the Plymouth Colony to trade with the Dutch colonists from New Amsterdam (New York City) via Buzzards Bay.

Less than two decades after settling Plymouth Colony, the English leaders established the Aptucxet Trading Post in what is today's town of Bourne. Aptucxet or "little trap in the water," was already a place where native Wampanoag Indians had long gathered on the banks to fish and trade. Two English sentinels lived at the post full-time. They had a small garden, grew corn, and kept a few pigs. The English settlers traded items such as metal pots, iron tools, and linen goods they obtained from Europe. Fur pelts obtained from trade with native Indians were packed in barrels and shipped back to England for additional goods to trade. Beaver, muskrat, and otter were particularly valuable because of their resistance to water.

The Dutch merchant De Rasière sailed his sloops to the Aptucxet Trading Post, bringing the early settlers food and much needed supplies as well as additional goods to trade with the Indians. To facilitate three-way trading, De Rasière suggested using wampum, or small beads of polished quahog shells, as a medium of exchange. Although the native Indians benefitted by trade, the trading post allowed the English colonists to gain control of land and commerce. It's not known how long the Aptucxet Trading Post operated, but this first commercial venture in North America is thought to have continued until the 1660s. All that remains of the original structure is the stone foundation. The town of Bourne reconstructed the building in 1930 with meticulous attention to historic detail. Open seasonally to visitors, it provides a rich look into the first settlement on Cape Cod.

The structure that exists today is a replica of the Aptucxet Trading Post. It was built on the original foundation uncovered in 1926.

Aptucxet Trading Post, 2008, oil on panel, 9 x 12.

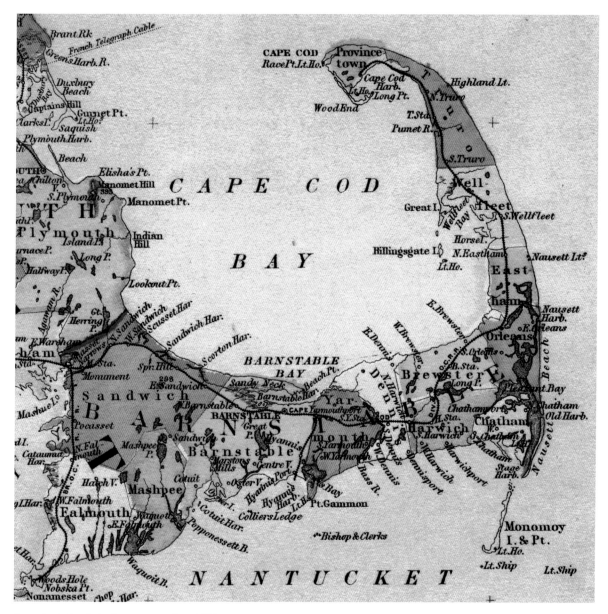

Cape Cod. Frank A. Gray, map author, 1881.

CHAPTER THREE
ESTABLISHING TOWNS

Most of the people who settled the Cape (and later the Islands) were not technically
separatists like the Pilgrims, but various splinter groups from Massachusetts Bay Colony.
—Paul Schneider, The Enduring Shore

Introduction

In the years following the establishment of Plymouth Colony, as more families arrived from England, available land was quickly taken. Colonists from other New England towns like Lynn and Scituate were also looking for better areas to settle. The Aptucxet trading post, erected in Bourne, made Cape Cod, particularly nearby Sandwich, an ideal choice. After William Bradford received the patent from the Earl of Warwick in 1630, annexing the whole of the Cape to the Plymouth colony, the way opened for expansion. At first, some thought of moving the entire Plymouth colony to Nauset, today's Eastham, the area that *Mayflower* scouts first explored. However, its remoteness fifty miles away and unsuitable harbor, particularly considering future growth, were deterrents.

It's easy to be confused by the assortment of municipal names on Cape Cod. Before considering the settlement of each Cape town, a few words of clarification. Primarily four towns, Sandwich, Barnstable, Yarmouth, and Eastham, formed the origins of all other Cape towns with the exception of Provincetown. The broader geographic areas of the Cape are known as Upper-Cape, Mid-Cape, Lower-Cape, and Outer-Cape. Within these divisions are fifteen towns which make up the County of Barnstable. Within each town there are villages which may number few or many. The following sections give a glimpse of each town in the order of their geographic location starting with the Upper-Cape.

Upper-Cape

Sandwich

Sandwich was the first town established on the Cape in 1637. Myles Standish and John Alden, names familiar to all school children, partnered to survey the land and determine boundary lines. Close to both Plymouth Colony and Aptucxet Trading Post, and with extensive marshes of salt hay providing abundant free fodder for livestock made Sandwich very attractive for settlement. A nearby stream was a valuable source of water and ideal, if dammed, to provide power for a grist mill. Edmund Freeman along with nine other men from Saugus (now Lynn, Massachusetts) was given permission by Governor Bradford to take enough land for 60 families. Over the first year about twenty-five families from Lynn, Duxbury, and Plymouth joined them. In the early days Sandwich was primarily an agricultural town and farmers also raised cattle and sheep. Officially incorporated in 1639, it was named Sandwich after the home town in Kent, England. The town motto is "Post Tot Naufracia Portus," Latin for "after so many shipwrecks a haven." The original Dexter Grist Mill was built around 1640. In time, a tannery con-verted animal skins into clothing and shoes, a blacksmith shop made tools, and many small businesses opened.

Much later, The Boston and Sandwich Glass Company, which opened in 1825, brought economic prosperity to the town. The factory employed over 500 workers at its peak and Sandwich gained national recognition for its glassworks. The Keith and Ryder Wagon Factory also boosted the manufacturing base of the area. A workers' strike and competition from mid-western plants caused the glass factory to close its doors in 1888. Sandwich survived its period of decline and, today, remains a charming town. Much of its appeal is due to the town's resistance to permitting businesses that would detract from its quaint New England character. Around the early 1960s both the ancient Dexter Grist Mill and Hoxie House (c.1640) were restored. These buildings, along with the impressive Town Hall built in 1834 are located on historic Shawme Pond and constitute the heart of the town's historic district. The town of Sandwich includes the villages of East Sandwich and Forestdale.

Sandwich Village, 2004, oil on canvas panel, 11 x 14.
Little has changed in the heart of historic Sandwich village over the last century. The Sandwich Glass Museum, Dexter Grist Mill, and Hoxie House remind the visitor of the town's rich past. Shawme Pond, dotted with graceful willow trees, is a storybook setting with swans and geese gliding by.

Bourne

The rapid development of West Sandwich (now Bourne) and the rail line which connected the Buzzards Bay side to off-Cape markets led to discord. In 1884, the town of Sandwich split and Bourne was incorporated as a separate entity. Ironically, Bourne was the last town on the Cape to be incorporated, yet it has the earliest history. Governor William Bradford visited "Manomet," as it was then called, and helped establish the Aptucxet Trading Post in 1627. Named after Jonathon Bourne, a state legislator and the town's most successful owner of whaling ships, the town began as a patchwork of villages. Today there are eight: Bourne Village, Buzzards Bay, Sagamore, Sagamore Beach, Bournedale, Pocasset, Cataumet and Monument Beach. Initially an agricultural and fishing community, the town boomed in the 1800s with factories, mills, and wharves for shipbuilding. The Keith Car (railroad) Works (formerly Keith and Ryder Wagon Factory when it was in Sandwich) in Sagamore Village was the largest manufacturing plant on the Cape in 1922.

The magnificent shoreline along Buzzards Bay attracted summer visitors early on. President Grover Cleveland established a summer home there which he named *Gray Gables*. It became the summer White House during the second term of his presidency. Although moved from its original location, the railroad station especially built for him still exists and sits next to the Aptuexet Trading Post. The arrival of the railroad to Buzzards Bay in 1848 spawned a growing tourist industry. Affluent summer visitors built elegant sprawling estates along the shores of the bay. One of the most significant events for the town of Bourne was the completion of the Cape Cod Canal in 1914. This inland waterway would provide safe passage for ships from all parts of the world, eliminating passage over the treacherous coastal shoals and waters of the North Atlantic. The Bourne and Sagamore Bridges, which span the man-made waterway, make Bourne the "first town on Cape Cod" for visitors. The Massachusetts Maritime Academy, the nation's oldest continually operating maritime academy, moved from Boston to Bourne in 1948. Bourne Village with its meticulously restored buildings, a blacksmith shop, and the Aptucxet Trading Post all provide today's visitor a splendid sense of its people and places of historical significance.

Falmouth

Settlement after Sandwich flowed eastward to the Mid-Cape with Yarmouth and Barnstable being the next towns to be established. However, one group moved south. In 1660 some of the settlers from Barnstable sailing west along Vineyard Sound came to an area with hills, fertile lands and an expansive shoreline. It was called Suckanesset, translated as "the place of black shells" by the native Wampanoags. These first colonists were families fleeing religious repression: Quakers who would settle in the western region and Congregationalists who would establish themselves in the central area. Soon, they were followed by colonists from Plymouth, Sandwich, and Barnstable. The town was incorporated in 1686 and the name changed to Falmouth in 1693 after the English port in Cornwall.

Like other Cape towns, Falmouth has produced many mariners, whalers, and shipbuilders. At one point, half of the 300 homes in Falmouth were owned by sea captains. The town was also an important agricultural community. Cranberries, strawberries, and "good English hay" were cultivated. In the early 1800s, Falmouth led all strawberry production east of the Mississippi. With the introduction of Merino sheep and beginnings of water-driven mills to process the wool, sheep husbandry became popular. Falmouth men championed several skirmishes with the British. When a British landing party attempted to come ashore during the American Revolution, heavy gunfire held them back. Later, in the War of 1812, the British ship *HMS Nimrod* came into the harbor and the captain ordered townspeople to turn over their cannons. Although under heavy fire, Falmouth soldiers were able to fight off the attack.

Bordered by Vineyard Sound and Buzzards Bay, with an expansive shoreline, Falmouth became the Cape's first summer colony for the wealthy. Beaches were more protected and the water warmer on Nantucket Sound as opposed to bay waters on the north coast. Daniel Webster, in a letter to a friend, described the town as "the handsomest place in these regions." Today's Shining Sea Bikeway honors Katharine Lee Bates, author of the song, *America the Beautiful*, who was born in Falmouth in 1859. The town, known to have been a summer colony for "free thinkers," is where Louis Aggasiz founded a research colony in 1888 that ultimately became the world famous Marine Biological Laboratory. In 1930, the Rockefeller Foundation bestowed $3 million to found the Woods Hole Oceanographic Institution. Falmouth is comprised of the villages of East Falmouth, Hatchville, Teaticket, Waquoit, North Falmouth, Silver Beach, West Falmouth and Woods Hole.

Falmouth Village, 2003, oil on canvas panel, 16 x 20.
Well maintained homes, shade trees and gardens line Falmouth's Main Street. The business district with its brick sidewalks, street lamps and abundant plantings lure visitors. One can easily imagine a less hurried Victorian age with couples leisurely strolling.

Mashpee

Wampanoag Indians inhabited the territory originally known as Massipee or "land near the great pond" for at least 10,000 years. Situated between the towns of Barnstable and Falmouth, it is bordered by Vineyard Sound on the south and Poponesset Bay on the east and includes the village of New Seabury. Captain Myles Standish was first to negotiate the acquisition of land in Mashpee "for use of the inhabitants of Barnstable." For two kettles and a bushel of corn, he acquired the areas known to this day as Cotuit and Santuit. The native Indians, having no appreciation of the concept of permanent ownership, continued to hunt and set up homes. This was the case in other Cape territories as well and friction with the settlers developed. Sandwich resident Richard Bourne was sympathetic to the Indians and in 1664 petitioned the General Court at Plymouth for natives to be allowed to form a government to manage their own affairs and establish land rights. He was keenly aware of the settlers' avid acquisition of new land and tried to protect the Mashpee Indians from infringement by the English.

Two decades later Bourne's son Shearjashub, built a meetinghouse for the Indians that still stands. In 1685, continuing his father's work, he convinced the Plymouth Court to confer title of the land in Mashpee to "South Sea [as the area was known] Indians" and their children forever. From then on, no land could be sold to English people without the consent of all the Indians. Sadly in 1693, less than a decade later, this settlement was undone when new laws removed many of the natives' civil rights and once again allowed legal confiscation of the land by white settlers. In 1861, legislation gave the Indians full citizenship and in 1870, Mashpee was incorporated as a town. Today, although the Wampanoag tribe has evolved in many ways, it remains true to tribal customs. It keeps sacred traditions alive and shares them with the public at the annual Wampanoag Tribal Pow Wow. The three-day event celebrates the activities, dance and music of Cape Cod's native people.

Southwest view of the Indian church in Mashpee. Drawing by J.W. Barber, engraved by S. E. Brown, c.1839. *Courtesy Nickerson Archives, Cape Cod Community College.*

Mid-Cape

Yarmouth

The second town on the Cape established after Sandwich was Mattacheese, also called Mattacheeset, translated "old lands by the borders of water" in the native tongue. The lands had long been settled by the Mattakeese and Nobscusset tribes of the Wampanoag nation. After several failed attempts by others at building homes, Anthony Thacher, John Crowe, and Thomas Howes settled the town in 1639. By 1640, Mattacheese had been renamed Yarmouth, probably after Great Yarmouth in England. The first generations of Yarmouth settlers, including its three founders, were farmers. Unlike the early settlers in Plymouth, those in Yarmouth enjoyed abundant food staples with plentiful vegetable and corn crops.

Dissention over land rights existed from the beginning. Committees were appointed to settle matters, but they couldn't put the discontent to rest until Captain Myles Standish was appointed to "have a hearing and put an end to all differences." Deyo's *History of Barnstable County, Massachusetts* relates,

The fiery captain showed the same pluck and decision in this matter that he exhibited in warlike exploits, and adopted decidedly heroic remedies. Many parties were ejected from lands claimed and occupied by them. Most of the former grants were abrogated and the lands reverted to the possession of the town. They were then reassigned agreeably to the views of the commissioner. There was no appeal, and smothering their resentment as best they might, the townsmen submitted from compulsion. Thus was ended one of the potent causes of internal discontent in the community.

In 1713 a reservation in South Yarmouth was set aside for native Wampanoag use. Unfortunately, by 1763 most of the Indian population was wiped out. Information from the Historical Society of Old Yarmouth tells us that the former "Indian lands" were sold and the one remaining native, Thomas Greenough, leased his lands to a David Kelley. Today there is a stone memorial dedicated to the last Wampanoags on a hillside near Long Pond on Indian Memorial Drive in South Yarmouth.

Kelley, a prominent Quaker, then bought up much of the land to build what would be known as "Friends Village." Other churches were also established, first by the Baptists and then by the Methodists. But it was the Quakers who established the business and social structure of the town.

Although Yarmouth was primarily a farming community in the 18th century, it also became known for its maritime activities. Packet ships lined the shores on both sides of the town, as did rows of salt works. Many Yarmouth sea captains were involved in the Indo-China trade. Present day tourists get a sense of Yarmouth's rich and varied past when visiting its two historic districts. Many of the buildings are on the National Register of Historic Places and reflect varied architectural styles: Federal, Victorian, Greek Revival, and, of course, the traditional Cape Cod house. Yarmouth was the parent town from which Harwich, Dennis, Brewster, and Chatham would later split off.

Eastern view of Yarmouth. Drawing by J.W. Barber, engraved by S. E. Brown, c.1839. *Courtesy Nickerson Archives, Cape Cod Community College.*

Barnstable

The town of Barnstable was settled in 1639, only a few months after Yarmouth. Unlike the Yarmouth settlers, who had come from diverse backgrounds, early white settlers in Barnstable were members of a flock of united followers of the Reverend John Lothrop. A Congregational minister, Lothrop had been persecuted and imprisoned in England before immigrating to America with twenty-five followers. The group originally settled in Scituate. According to Amos Otis in *Genealogical Notes of Barnstable Families*, after petitioning Governor Thomas Prence in Plymouth for a place that "to the end God might have the more glorye and wee (we) more comfort," than Scituate, they arrived in Barnstable on October 11, 1639. Within three years, they had their dwellings built and Lothrop's home, completed in 1644, served as the meeting house where he preached his sermons. This building, one of the oldest on Cape Cod, is now part of the Sturgis Public Library in Barnstable Village. Named after William Sturgis, a direct descendant of Reverend Lothrop, it is the oldest building housing a public library in the United States. It also has the distinction of being the oldest structure in America where religious services were once held.

Barnstable Village, 2004, oil on canvas, 18 x 24.
Entering Barnstable Village from the west on Old King's Highway, one passes the Olde Colonial Courthouse and the Sturgis Library, on the left. Opposite on the south side of the street is the Crocker Tavern, a former stagecoach stop. Further along on the south side of Main Street is the majestic Barnstable County Courthouse. This Greek Revival building, listed on the National Register of Historic Places dominates the town from its throne atop a knoll. On the courthouse front lawn, facing the water, are two cannons installed to prevent attacks from British Ships. Somehow they never needed to be fired as the sand bars in the harbor proved effective deterrents.

Barnstable, like other Cape towns was primarily colonized by farmers. In addition to livestock, they raised corn, rye, onions, and flax. By the 1800s, fishing, shipping, and coastal trading drove the economy. By the end of the nineteenth century, there were some 800 ships harbored in the town. Over one hundred shipmasters claimed the village of Centerville as home. The Crosby Boatyard in Osterville is famous for designing the Cape Cod catboat. During World War II the Army Corps of Engineers took control of the Crosby property in order to conduct landing boat training for the Normandy invasion.

The town of Barnstable is comprised of seven villages: Hyannis, West Barnstable, Barnstable Village, Marstons Mills, Cotuit, Osterville, and Centerville. Barnstable Village continues to be the county seat. Village homes and businesses were built along an ancient, curving Indian trail situated a short distance inland. It is known today as Old Kings Highway or the less prosaic Route 6A. This road, following hilly contours, takes one past historic homes, charming shops and the scenic harbor. It extends all the way to Provincetown. Hyannis is the primary business center for Cape Cod.

Main Street, Centerville, 2005, oil on canvas 18 x 24.
Stately sea captain homes, well tended gardens and shade trees line Centerville's Main Street suggesting the town's prosperous maritime past. Named for its central location among the other villages in Barnstable County, Centerville was formerly called Chequaquet or "pleasant harbor" by the native Wampanoags.

Dennis

The town of Dennis split off from Yarmouth and was incorporated as a town in 1793 and named in honor of Reverend Josiah Dennis, the first minister who came to preach in the church. Many of the settlers were farmers in England and were attracted to the area by the abundant salt marsh hay that provided food and bedding for their livestock. The colonists quickly became aware of the worth of drift whales that beached on their shores. Harvesting and selling the valuable oil boosted the early economy. When the supply of beached whales diminished, Dennis men sought them offshore. Never able to compete with Nantucket when the whaling industry expanded, the townsmen turned to shore fishing, shipbuilding, and coastal trading. In the mid 19th century, the Shiverick Shipyard in East Dennis built eight of the mighty clipper ships that ruled the Golden Age of Sail. Two of the best known were the *Wild Hunter* and the *Belle of the West*. These vessels went to all corners of the world to trade cargo that included silk, tea, lumber, and fertilizer. Most of the captains were Dennis men and they brought fame and fortune to the town. In all, four hundred shipmasters called Dennis home.

Innovators in Dennis spawned two other major Cape industries: cranberry cultivation and saltworks. Henry Hall of North Dennis noticed that when sand blew over wild cranberries, the crop yields increased. Creating similar conditions on his bog, he ultimately produced enough cranberries to sell to the Boston market. John Sears of East Dennis directed his ingenuity at inventing a new way to harvest salt from the ocean. His method of solar evaporation replaced the inefficient boiling of sea water. As in much of Cape Cod, the arts thrive in today's Dennis. It is home to the Cape Cod Museum of Art, Cape Playhouse, and Cape Cinema. All are located in a pleasant compound just off Old Kings Highway. The town of Dennis includes the villages of Dennis Port, Dennis Village (North Dennis), East Dennis, South Dennis and West Dennis.

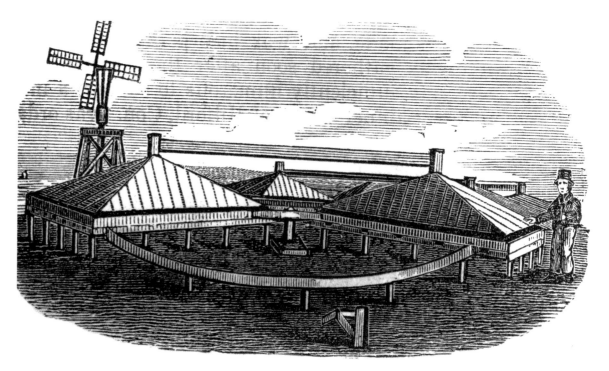

Dennis apparatus used in making salt.
Drawing by J.W. Barber, engraved by S. E. Brown, c.1839. *Courtesy Nickerson Archives, Cape Cod Community College.*

Harwich

Harwich was settled as a plantation of old-comers (a name referring to original Plymouth settlers) after the Plymouth colony relinquished its charter and was absorbed into the Massachusetts Bay Colony. Large parcels of land were purchased from remaining Wampanoags. In time, these lots would divide and form today's towns of Harwich, Brewster, Chatham, Orleans and Eastham. By 1690 there were enough settlers to hire a minister, and four years later, Harwich became officially incorporated as a town. Early settlers were predominantly farmers and the economy was agriculturally based. Later, it would become one of Cape Cod's major fishing ports. Those who first went to sea did not have to go very far since a large population of whales frequented Cape Cod Bay. As the whales retreated to undisturbed deeper waters, local whalers sought them on sloops, then graduated to schooners.

After the Revolutionary War, the fishing industry in Harwich centered on cod and mackerel, this time on the southern coast of the town. In Deyo's *History of Barnstable County, Massachusetts*, it states,

> In 1802, between fifteen and twenty vessels, averaging forty tons each, and about half of them owned here, were employed in shoal fishing, and four, of about one hundred tons each, in fishing on the banks of Newfoundland and in the straits of Belle Isle. It was estimated that over two hundred persons, including men and boys, were engaged at this time in the cod fishing from this place.

Toward the latter part of the 19th century when larger ships required deeper harbors, the fishing industry in Harwich declined. Many sea captains and retired fishermen turned to cranberry cultivation to support their families. Two Harwich men, Captain Alvin Cahoon and his cousin, Captain Cyrus Cahoon experimented and developed improved methods of cultivation. By the early 1850s, Harwich became the largest producer of cranberries on the Cape. At that time a five-acre cranberry bog could provide a comfortable income for a family.

After John Sears from Dennis devised the method of solar evaporation to produce salt from sea water, another two men from Harwich gave that industry a major boost. Nathaniel Freeman suggested the use of windmills as a device to pump in the seawater to the evaporating troughs. Reuben Sears invented a roof that could be easily rolled on and off the evaporating bins to protect the concentrating salt from rain.

Lower-Cape

Brewster

Incorporated in 1803, Brewster was originally established as the north parish of Harwich. Divisive feelings existed for some time between the northern district, mostly populated by prosperous sea captains and the south, home to farmers and fishermen. When the towns split, the southern area retained the name Harwich. The north situated Brewster was named in honor of *Mayflower* passenger Elder William Brewster, the first religious leader of the Pilgrims at Plymouth. It's been said that more shipmasters sailed from Brewster than any other town in the country. In the 1840s, a Brewster youth would be looked down upon if he didn't go to sea as soon as his schooling was complete. Many who ventured out went on to captain their own vessels. Sometimes two or three men got together to share ownership. Joseph C. Lincoln in his foreword to *Brewster Ship Masters* writes,

> *Sea captains? Why, there were none but sea captains, or the wives and children of sea captains, in Brewster of old. It was practically certain and safe to hail an adult Brewster citizen by the title, "Cap'n." Cap'n Snow kept the village grocery, Cap'n Foster was chairman of selectmen, Cap'n Baker endowed the library, Cap'n Nickerson's donation repaired and painted the meetinghouse, and of that meetinghouse, deacons and pew holders, sexton and choir-leader, indeed, every male but the minister himself, was captain.*

Their legacy is reflected in the beautiful old mansions that still remain, although many have since been converted to inns.

In 1663 Governor Thomas Prence of Plymouth ordered a water-powered grist mill built in Brewster along Stony Brook Pond. He hoped a corn-grinding mill would attract more homesteaders to the area. Enough people came so that in two years a fulling mill (a mill that cleaned and shrunk homemade wool cloth) was built across the road and shared the brook's waterpower. In the mid-1830s there would also be a tannery, cotton weaving mill, and paper mill. The original Stony Brook mill burned down completely in 1871 due to a fire caused by the miller who was making smoked herring inside the mill. It

was rebuilt two years later and is the mill one sees today. In 1940, the town of Brewster acquired the property which includes a herring run, grist mill, and remains of the factory village.

The Cape Cod Museum of Natural History on Route 6A in Brewster is the place to start if one is interested in learning about the Cape's natural environment. It offers nature trails, guided walks and kayak tours, as well as a full range of wildlife exhibits, and presentations. Henry David Thoreau, over a century ago, lauded the beauty of Brewster in his journal: "In short, Brewster, with its noble ponds, its bare hills . . . and secluded cottages, is a very interesting town to an inlanders." For those who prefer the indoors, the Brewster Ladies' Library provides a vast selection of reading material and two lovely historic parlors in which to settle and read.

Southeastern view of Brewster (central part). Drawing by J.W. Barber, engraved by S. E. Brown, c.1839. *Courtesy Nickerson Archives, Cape Cod Community College.*

Chatham

Fifteen years before the Pilgrims dropped anchor at Provincetown, the French explorer Samuel de Champlain anchored in Stage Harbor with hopes of founding New France there. In skirmishes with the Indians, four of his men were killed. The problems with the natives, along with navigating the difficult shoals around Monomoy, discouraged him and his fellow explorers from establishing a permanent settlement. They sailed away leaving an opening for later English settlement. Fifty years after that, William Nickerson from Yarmouth began more civil dealings with the Indians and, through trade, accumulated large parcels of land in the area for his extensive family. Although his transactions were disputed by authorities in Plymouth Colony, after lengthy negotiations, he paid a fine, and later obtained a written deed for the land — some 4,000 acres.

By the 1700s, Monomoy, as Chatham was then called, was still little advanced beyond a neighborhood of Nickerson families who farmed the land. It was not incorporated as a town until 1712, when the Reverend Hugh Adams became the resident minister. The town's name was inspired by the river port town of Chatham in Kent, England. Prior to the Revolutionary War, the town was slow to develop. Its remote location and shoreline, susceptible to French privateers and British warships, discouraged settling. Over time, colonists established farms and cultivated corn, rye, wheat, and tobacco. Farming remained a mainstay, but by the mid-1700s the fishing industry, salt works, and shipbuilding began to develop. Along with Harwich and Barnstable, Chatham relied on fishing, bringing in shiploads of cod, halibut, and mackerel from local waters and the Grand Banks.

The thriving maritime economy came to a standstill with the Revolutionary War. The English blockaded all Cape ports and Chatham's ships rotted in the harbor for most of the war. After the war, Chatham's situation improved. Industries such as ship building, salt production, and fish exportation gave the economy a boost. Whaling and other maritime enterprises flourished adding fortunes to the town and its population. Early travel to Chatham was tedious and possible only by boat or stagecoach. The establishment of the railroad to Chatham in 1887 made travel easier and more comfortable. Wealthy families from New York and Boston began to vacation there and purchase summer homes. What was once a liability for settlement became a welcoming attraction: a remotely beautiful place with great exposure to the ocean.

Chatham Twins, 2003, oil on canvas panel, 16 x 20. Chatham is the only town on Cape Cod with a working lighthouse in the center of its village. The stately light station stands guard over magnificent Chatham beach.

Orleans

Known to the Pilgrims by its native name, Nauset, Orleans was first settled in 1642 by Nicholas Snow and his family while it was still a southern precinct of Eastham. Seeking independence since 1717, it finally broke away from Eastham and was incorporated as a separate town in 1797. The origin of the name is believed to honor Louis Philippe II, the Duke of Orleans, in recognition of France's support for the thirteen colonies during the American Revolution. Although Orleans is a coastal town, shipbuilding was never developed as an industry. Only one 70 ton schooner was built before 1800 and there were only 33 fishing vessels in service. The packet business, however, was extensive with boats carrying cargo and passengers between Orleans and Boston.

Salt manufacturing began around 1800, and was carried on for many years by a number of enterprising citizens. In 1837, fifty saltworks made 21,780 bushels of salt. Orleans is connected to France by more than its name. From 1890 to 1959 a key communications link between the United States and Europe was a 3,200-mile underwater cable from Orleans to Brest, France. It was the United States' only source for daily stock transactions and news from Europe for 50 years until the advent of the wireless radio. Noteworthy messages were transmitted to the world: The 1898 sinking of the steamer *Portland* off the stormy coast of Cape Cod with hundreds of lives lost; Lindbergh's 1927 successful trans-Atlantic solo flight to Paris. "Les Boches sont ici - the Germans are here," gave notice of Germany's invasion and occupation of France in 1940. It took about five minutes for messages to go back and forth across the ocean. The Orleans station operated until it was dismantled by the U.S. Signal Corps during World War II. It was put back into operation in 1952, and finally closed in November 1959. The final message sent out on the line was, "Have a happy Thanksgiving. Station closed." In 1972 a committee of ten prominent Orleans residents raised money to purchase the cable station from France. It was opened as a public museum in July 1972.

Several of the most significant events in Orleans history actually took place off its shores. During the war of 1812, the captain of the British vessel, *H.M.S. Newcastle* anchored in Rock Harbor and threatened to destroy the town's saltworks unless he was paid a $1,000 ransom. The offer was refused and when the British sailors attempted to land, the Orleans Militia successfully drove them away. A little over a century later, in the summer of 1918, a German U-boat surfaced off Nauset Beach during World War I. It fired on the *Perth Amboy*, an unarmed tug boat, and the four barges it was pulling. At least one of the shells fired from the sub landed on the beach, making this the only assault on the United States during World War I. Pilots in three planes from the Chatham Air Station launched a counterattack, but the submarine escaped.

Town Cove, Orleans, 2005, oil on canvas panel, 12 x 24.
Aaron Snow built a Victorian mansion on Town Cove in 1875. He operated a store from the lower level of the house. Considered pretentious, it was called "Aaron's Folly," by more modest townspeople. Today it houses the lovely Orleans Waterfront Inn.

Outer-Cape

Eastham

Eastham, originally named Nauset, was one of the four original towns established on Cape Cod. In the early 1640s when the Plymouth Colony had become overcrowded and land was no longer agriculturally viable, there was initial interest in moving the entire colony to Nauset. Although the plan was never carried out, large tracts of land were bought from the Indians and many settlers did come to Eastham. Led by Governor Thomas Prence, the town grew rapidly and was incorporated in 1646. Five years later the court ordered "that the town of Nauset be henceforth called and known as Eastham."

In 1654 the western part of Eastham was given to some settlers who by virtue of being "old comers" or Pilgrims who arrived on the first three boats (*Mayflower, Fortune, Ann*) and had claim to the area. Reverend Samuel Treat of Milford, Connecticut, became Eastham's minister in 1672. He became distinguished for his evangelical zeal not only among English settlers, but the native tribes as well. He learned their language, visited their dwellings, and won their trust and affection, converting many to Christianity. At that time there were 500 adult native Indians in the town who attended public worship. By 1764, this number had dwindled to only four individuals, the rest having succumbed to fatal diseases.

In the early decades of settlement, Eastham was primarily an agricultural community. Grain production was abundant enough to allow Eastham to export it. The soil was particularly well suited for growing asparagus and turnips. However, over-farming and strong winds depleted and removed much of the top soil. In time, the community turned to the sea for fishing and salt making. Eastham's summer resort history began as early as 1830 when the Methodist Church established a summer camp meeting ground in town. These camp meetings became all the rage and every August thousands would gather in Eastham's Millennium Grove to hear as many as 150 different ministers preach. Author and naturalist, Henry Beston, recorded his observations of the great beach on Eastham's Atlantic shore for his 1928 classic book, *The Outermost House: A Year of Life on the Great Beach of Cape Cod*. Today, Eastham's fame is derived from its being the gateway to the National Seashore.

Ancient pear tree in Eastham. Drawing by J.W. Barber, engraved by S. E. Brown, c.1839. *Courtesy Nickerson Archives, Cape Cod Community College.*

Wellfleet

Although the first permanent settlement in Wellfleet was in 1650, the town did not attain official status until 1763. The first settlers were primarily subsistence farmers. Although Eastham, Wellfleet's next door neighbor, was a thriving farming community, agriculture never developed on a large scale in the latter town. Wellfleet's sandy soil, after being cleared for planting, quickly eroded into barren sand dunes. Its harbor on the other hand, was known for abundant shellfish even before the area was formally settled. The town's name is felt to be derived from a location on the English coast of Essex near the Thames. A stretch of shellfish beds there yielded particularly large and delectable bivalves; they were called "Walflete" oysters.

When an epidemic in 1770 killed off the oyster beds, Wellfleet men turned to commercial fishing and lobstering. After the Revolutionary War, Wellfleet ultimately became one of the leading cod and mackerel fishing ports in Massachusetts. Shell fishermen from Connecticut and Maryland would ship oysters to Wellfleet to be planted in the harbor to acquire the famous Wellfleet flavor and then re-harvest them for selling in the Boston Market.

Salt making was also a big industry. During the 1830s there were some 40 saltworks producing 18,000 bushels of salt annually. Mackerel fishing started to decline around 1880 and by 1900 there were no longer any boats sailing from Wellfleet Harbor.

In 1901, when Guglielmo Marconi sought a clear view across the ocean to build a wireless communication station, he chose a cliff overlooking the Atlantic Ocean in South Wellfleet. History was made on January 18, 1903 when a message from President Theodore Roosevelt was telegraphed to the Wellfleet site and then transmitted to King Edward VII at Poldhu, on the south Cornish coast of England. Unlike other Cape towns that have seen burgeoning residential and commercial growth, over 60 percent of Wellfleet's 13,000 acres are protected and restricted as a result of the establishment in 1961 of the Cape Cod National Seashore. Native oysters as well as quahogs, clams, and scallops remain an important part of the town's economy. The Wellfleet "Oysterfest" each October celebrates its prized local product and draws thousands of visitors into the town.

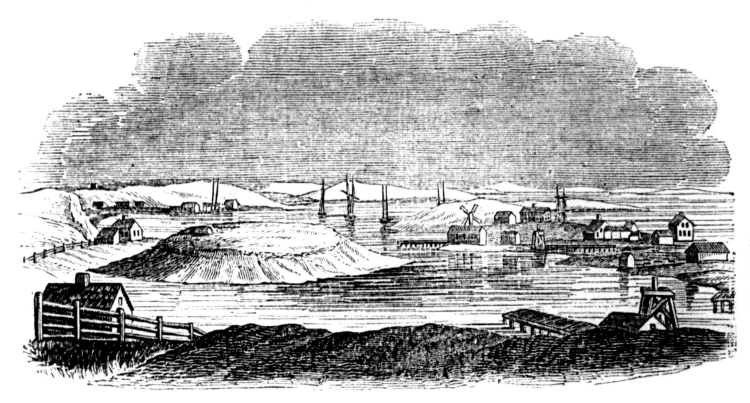

Northern view of Wellfleet. Drawing by J.W. Barber, engraved by S. E. Brown, c.1839. Courtesy Nickerson Archives, Cape Cod Community College.

Truro

The area originally known as Pamet, was one of the places explorers from the *Mayflower* first considered for settlement. Although they decided to look further, the cache of native seed corn they unearthed proved critical for the Pilgrim's first planting in Plymouth. The area is known today as Corn Hill. In 1689 a group called the Pamet Proprietors agreed to purchase land from the native Indians living there. Pamet was established in 1705 and the name briefly changed to Dangerfield as a nod to the hazardous surrounding waters. In 1709 Dangerfield separated from Eastham, became incorporated as a town, and the name was changed to Truro after the English town in Cornwall. Initially farming was the basic way of life, but because of the scarcity of good soil, the settlers quickly turned to the sea. Shore whaling was done at first, followed by deep water whaling.

Small shipbuilding, fishing, and saltworks brought prosperity to Truro. From 1845 to 1852 fifteen schooners were built there, with most of the lumber from local forests. Gardens provided ample produce, and the sandy soil resulted in crops of asparagus and turnips large enough for shipment to the Boston markets. The creation of the National Seashore in 1960 has preserved almost two-thirds of Truro in its natural state. The inland hilltops overlook some of the finest ocean views on the east coast.

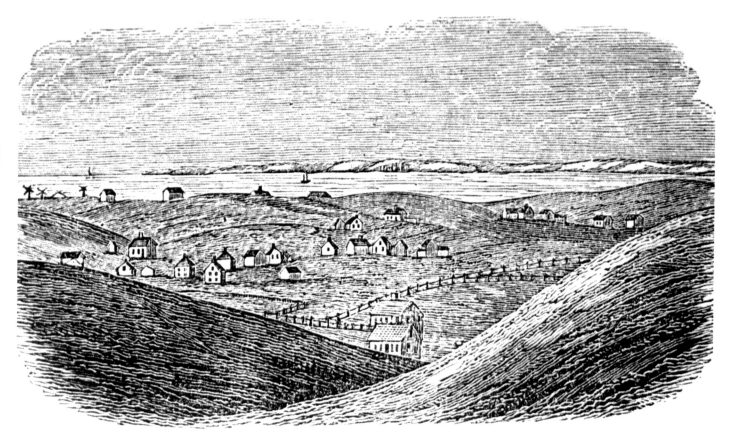

Eastern View of Pond Village Truro. Drawing by J.W. Barber, engraved by S. E. Brown, c.1839. Courtesy Nickerson Archives, Cape Cod Community College.

Provincetown

The towering Pilgrim Monument in the heart of Provincetown commemorates the Pilgrims' first landing in the New World. While the *Mayflower* anchored in Provincetown harbor for five weeks, the newcomers explored the areas now known as Truro, Wellfleet, and Eastham before sailing on to Plymouth. Although it harbored ships for more than a century, Provincetown was not incorporated as a town until 1727. During the 1700s, it was primarily a fishing village with a small population. The sandy, curving spit of land and its people remained under the control of the Plymouth Colony and later the Commonwealth. The fact that this tip of the Cape was a separate entity was reflected by its name "Provincelands." A small measure of compensation to those who lived there was exemption from military service and taxation.

After the American Revolution, the town grew rapidly as a fishing and whaling center. At its height, it boasted seventy-five wharves and was third, behind New Bedford and Nantucket in whaling. In his book, *Becoming Cape Cod*, James C. O'Connell writes that at the crest of Cape Cod's maritime activity, Provincetown was "the wealthiest town per capita in Massachusetts." While populations of other Cape towns declined after the Civil War, Provincetown's peaked at 4,642 in 1890. Portuguese fishermen, who came to the area to live and work on the ships, significantly increased the population and added a special flavor.

When the 1898 Portland Gale, as the storm is now known, hit the Cape Cod coast, Provincetown boats were severely damaged, many of the wharfs washed away, and buildings were left in ruins. Those who relied on the fishing industry were forced to leave. At that same time, the allure of the seaside beauty and isolation began to attract painters and writers who took over the dilapidated structures. Artist Charles Hawthorne founded an art colony in 1899 when he established the Cape Cod School of Art. An old fishing shack was

transformed into the Wharf Theater. The career of American dramatist Eugene O'Neill was launched there with the premiere of his first play, *Bound East for Cardiff*. In 1942, Mary Heaton Vorse, in *Time and the Town* wrote, "People in Provincetown have always danced and sung. The Portuguese came early and brought with them their Latin gaiety and gusto for living." As a result of the influx of large numbers of the gay community around the 1970s, Provincetown has become one of the best-known gay summer resorts on the east coast. In 1978, the Provincetown Business Guild (PBG) was formed to promote gay tourism. Today more than 200 businesses belong to the PBG and Provincetown remains a village of tolerance and celebration.

Provincetown Rooftops c.1912, 2008, oil on canvas panel, 16 x 20. The tall masts are gone, but the lure of the sea, historic buildings, art community and festive atmosphere attract thousands of visitors to Provincetown each year.

CHAPTER FOUR
HARVESTING THE LAND

Early Cape Cod farmers knew the limitations and the goodness of their soils,
what they would produce, and that some crops could be better raised than others.
—Albert Perry Brigham, *Cape Cod and the Old Colony*

Introduction

Prior to the arrival of the English colonists, Cape Cod was shaded by vast forests of pine, spruce, hemlock, maple, and oak. The rising sea had fostered the grassy growth of expansive salt marshes. Wild blueberries, strawberries, cranberries, and grapes grew in luxurious abundance. The buried corn that Mayflower explorers discovered in Indian caches on the outer Cape was a good indicator of ample future crops of this important grain. From the very start, agriculture was the basic occupation of the colonists. The quality of Cape Cod soil was variable but the native Wampanoags taught the newcomers to grow squash, pumpkins, and beans. Corn was raised all over the Cape and crops of up to three thousand bushels per year were grown in Eastham. To a lesser extent, flax, barley, rye, and wheat were harvested. Low-growing apple trees nestled in the hillsides and filled kettle holes.

Settlers made efforts to enrich the soil with marine fertilizers such as crab shells and herring, but over time they could not compensate for continuous planting, which greatly diminished the fertility of the land. The quality of soil in Outer-Cape towns, such as Truro and Wellfleet, exposed to ocean winds and shifting sand dunes, was particularly affected. After the Civil War, as railroads developed, commodities from western lands were cheaper to import than they could be grown locally. By the early 1900s, Barnstable produced a meager two acres of wheat, sixteen acres of rye, and no barley. In time, Cape Codders would put their efforts into growing crops more suitable to the climate and soil. Although Cape Cod salt hay and cornfields are no longer harvested as they once were, their importance in local history endures. Fortunately, some unique crops associated with the Cape from colonial days endure and are still found naturally or farmed.

Salt Hay

In 1830 there was no cultivated hay at all due to a severe drought; it was only the unfailing abundance of salt hay that saved livestock from starving.
—Marise Fawsett, *Cape Cod Annals*

Gathering Salt Hay in Barnstable. c.1880 *Courtesy Nickerson Archives, Cape Cod Community College.*

One crop on Cape Cod that required no planting and was crucial to the colonists was marsh grass or salt hay (*Spartina patens*). It blanketed thousands of acres of land from Sandwich to Provincetown. Early settlers depended heavily on their animals: oxen for hauling heavy loads, cattle for food and milk, and sheep for wool and meat. All of these creatures had to be fed and fed a lot! Early settlers didn't know about minerals and vitamins, but they did know that their cattle survived the winter months on a diet of salt hay and were still fleshy in the spring. The expansive Cape Cod salt marshes were invaluable as a free and ever-growing source of food and bedding for these animals.

As years went by and land was cleared, hay would be cultivated, but marsh hay continued to be an important supplement. The animals could graze freely on the marshes in the spring and early summer, and then the farmers would harvest the winter's supply in August. It was hard, exhausting work. Heat in the open fields was extremely uncomfortable and green flies were everywhere. It could also be dangerous. Scythes were used to cut the hay and one careless move might slice an arm or leg.

Harvesting had to be timed with low tide so the marsh would be firm underfoot. "Bog shoes" or wooden platforms were clamped to the hooves of work animals so they didn't sink in the muck. The salt hay was stacked on "staddles," wooden platforms elevated from the ground by wooden poles. This means of storage allowed the farmer to harvest the hay before the next high tide and then return at will to take it to his farm, which might be miles away. It was not only a valued source of food for cattle, early colonists also stuffed dried salt hay into mattresses, stacked it against building foundations to provide insulation from the cold, and used it to thatch roofs.

Salt Haying on Cape Cod. c.1900 *Courtesy Nickerson Archives, Cape Cod Community College.*

Corn

Heap high the farmer's wintry hoard! Heap high the golden corn!
No richer gift has autumn poured from out her lavish horn.
—John Greenleaf Whittier, *The Corn Song*

Dexter Grist Mill, 2006, oil on canvas, 11 x 14.

Beyond its use as food, in early colonial days corn was utilized as barter in trade and even to compensate the minister for his services. No part of it was wasted. After kernels were removed, early farmers used stalks to feed cattle in the winter, husks to make mattresses, and cobs for jug stoppers and pipe bowls. Raising corn was one matter, but the arduous task of hand-grinding it was another. Rock hard, dried kernels had to be ground into meal or flour suitable for baking. A small amount might be handled with a mortar and pestle in the home, but a grist mill was essential to produce the amount needed for food and day-to-day transactions. Thus, building grist mills and finding capable millers was crucial for a town and its people to prosper. The job of a miller required skill, dedication, and hard work, but offered significant rewards to the right person. Millers were exempt from military duty, given generous plots of land, and were held in high esteem in the community. Typically, his payment was in barter: a portion of the kernels that the townspeople brought to be milled. Thomas Dexter Sr., one of the original ten men who settled Sandwich in 1637 accepted the responsibility of building a grist mill in that town and was rewarded with 26 acres of land.

The first water-driven Dexter Mill, built around 1641, was powered by water flowing through a dam built on a spring fed creek. The resulting body of water still exists today and is known as Shawme Pond. The mill was short-lived, as was Dexter's stay in town. He left soon after erecting it. The task of rebuilding was taken on by his son, Thomas Dexter Jr., in 1654. The current mill is a reconstruction built in 1961 with mill stones imported from France. It operates from May to October and bags of fresh ground cornmeal are available.

Dexter Grist Mill Interior. The hopper on the upper right feeds the corn down to the grinding stones.

More difficult to construct was the traditional Dutch-style wind-driven mill. There were only a few men on Cape Cod that had the skill to build them. In *Cape Cod: Its People and Their History,* Henry C. Kittredge writes, "The difficulty of finding men who could build them was so great that capitalists who wanted a mill found it easier to scour the Cape for an old one, and move it to the desired location, than to hunt up a millwright. Half the windmills on the Cape ended their days on new sites." Best known builders were Thomas Baxter and his two sons of West Yarmouth, and Thomas Paine. Paine was an Eastham resident and traveled from Barnstable to Truro building windmills.

Eastham Mill, 2008, oil on canvas panel, 8 x 10
The Eastham Mill is the oldest working windmill on Cape Cod. Thomas Paine built the mill in Plymouth in 1680. It was later moved to Eastham.

Following are a couple of recipes from the Dexter Grist Mill.
Courtesy of the Town of Sandwich.

Recipes

Cornmeal from the Dexter Grist Mill.

Cornbread

Mix together:
1 cup cornmeal
1 cup flour
1/4 cup sugar
1/2 teaspoon salt
4 teaspoons baking powder

Stir in:
1 cup milk
1 egg
1/2 cup water
1/4 cup soft shortening

Bake in greased muffin or loaf pan for 25 minutes at oven temperature of 425° F. This recipe may be varied according to individual taste. To make it lighter, use 1 1/4 cups flour, 3/4 cup cornmeal and 2 eggs.

Baked Indian Pudding

3 cups milk
4 tablespoons cornmeal
1/3 cup molasses
1/2 cup sugar
1 egg (beaten)
1/4 teaspoon salt
1/2 teaspoon ginger
1/2 teaspoon cinnamon
butter, size of walnut
1 cup milk

In a medium saucepan, heat the 3 cups of milk. When it begins to simmer, add the cornmeal and molasses. Stir constantly to avoid scorching and cook until the mixture thickens. Remove from heat and add remaining ingredients except milk. Mix thoroughly. Pour into buttered baking dish and bake 1/2 hour at 300° F. Pour one cup milk over pudding and continue baking for 2 hours. Serve with cream or ice cream.

Cranberries

*Young girls make enough at cranberry picking to pay for their year's
clothing and board themselves during the year.*
"Cranberries on Cape Cod," Hartford Times, September 28, 1891

Cape Cod's cranberry history began when the Indians introduced the Pilgrims to the crop in the early 1600s. Wampanoag legend says the cranberry was carried from heaven in the beak of a white dove as a gift from the Great Spirit. The dove dropped the berry into a bog where in time it grew abundantly. Native American tribes called cranberries *sassamanash* and *ibimi*, which both translate into "bitter berry." Colonists called them "crane-berry" because the blossom and stem resembled a crane's head and neck. Indeed a gift from God, cranberries were very important in the diets of the first English colonists. Having subsisted on a diet of salted meat and dry biscuits for many weeks, and lacking fresh fruit, many developed scurvy from a vitamin C deficiency. The berries, rich in this vitamin, were boiled or dried and added to sauces and baked goods. In addition, the Wampanoag Indians who had been using cranberries for hundreds of years taught the colonists about their medicinal properties. They could be brewed to make poultices for wounds and made into soothing teas to ease stomach problems and cleanse the urinary tract. Dye made from the berries provided crimson-tinted wool and cloth. A recipe for cranberry sauce first appeared in a Pilgrim cookbook in 1633.

Ready for Harvest, 2005, oil on canvas, 8 x 10.

By the end of the 17th century, cranberries, corn, and salt-cod were the "holy trinity" of Cape Cod cuisine. One of the staples of the colonial diet, cranberries were eaten at almost every meal paired with fish, fowl, and meat. On Cape Cod and the Islands, cranberries grew wild in bogs: shallow areas of clay, gravel, and peat where there was nearby water and sand. For almost 200 years, Cape Codders harvested cranberries from the wild. Sometimes there were only sparse and unpredictable crops. As the popularity of the berry grew, many towns passed laws limiting picking to townspeople. By the 18th century, residents had staked out their bogs and picking was a family affair. In 1816, Captain Henry Hall of Dennis became the first to cultivate the berry. He noticed that when sand blew on his cranberry bogs and settled on the vines, cranberry production increased. In the 1840s Harwich cousins, Alvin and Cyrus Cahoon, developed their own bogs in the Pleasant Lake area of that town. Working together the two men developed methods that led to large scale commercial cranberry production. Within ten years, Harwich was the leader with over one thousand acres dedicated to harvesting the ruby-toned berry.

Until around 1880 cranberries were picked by hand and furnished employment to many women and children. Invention of the cranberry scoop allowed a skillful worker to pick fifty bushels a day. In 1891, *The Hartford Times* reported,

> *There is an enormous cranberry crop. The Old Colony Railroad had, up to Saturday morning, carried between eighty and one hundred carloads of the blushing but acid berries to Boston from the Cape Cod region. The picking began last week Monday, and it takes nearly four weeks to harvest the crop. All the schools in that entire region were closed, and all hands, men, women, and children, went to work to gather the crop. It will be the same all this week.*

In the 1800s many sea captains and fishermen who owned marshy lands would turn them into cranberry bogs and upon retirement would still be able to support their families. A five-acre bog provided a comfortable income for a family in the 1850s. Today, although other regions in the nation surpass Cape Cod in production, lush crimson cranberry bogs are still very much a part of the Cape Cod economy.

Cranberry pickers on Forest Street in Harwich, c.1880. *Courtesy Harwich Historical Society.*

The first cranberry scoops introduced in the 1850's were wooden baskets with comb-like wooden teeth that would pull the berries off the vines into the basket.

Recipes

Old Fashioned Cranberry Tart

Mix together:
> 1 cup of whole cranberries
> 1/2 cup chopped pecans
> 1/4 cup sugar

In a separate bowl mix:
> 1 egg
> Scant 1/2 cup sugar
> 1/4 cup melted butter
> 1/2 cup flour, sifted with 1/2 teaspoon baking soda

Mix together:
> 1 teaspoon cinnamon
> 2 teaspoons sugar

Combine the first three ingredients and place in prepared pie pan. In a separate bowl, mix the second group of ingredients. Spread the second mixture over the berries. Sprinkle with cinnamon and sugar mixture. Bake at 350 degrees F. for 35 minutes. Serve warm with whipped cream or vanilla ice cream.

Old Fashioned Cranberry Tart

Strawberries

The picking season is from three to four weeks. Pickers are usually paid 2 cents a quart and a good picker will make from $3 to $4 a day. Five thousand quarts is considered a fair yield per acre for the section.
—Cape Cod and All the Pilgrim Land

Native Americans were known to have picked wild strawberries since 1643. They crushed them in a mortar and mixed them with meal to make strawberry bread. Three hundred years later, in *Cape Cod and All the Pilgrim Land*, published in June 1922, it boasts, "Cape Cod strawberries are destined to become as famous as her cranberries, her fishing, and her renown as a summer resort. One million quarts of them left her fields the past season! And the industry is still growing!" Falmouth was not only the largest strawberry producer on the Cape, but led New England in the magnitude of its industry. Marilyn Halter in *Between Race and Ethnicity: Cape Verdean American Immigrants: 1860-1965*, writes, "Natural conditions were favorable to growing a high quality berry. The sandy soil was easily worked but heavy enough to withstand drought. A mild winter climate did not subject the plants to excessive cold."

Most of the cultivation was done by hand. This included clearing the land, setting plants, placing runners, applying fertilizer, hoeing and weeding, and of course, picking. In the early 1900s the industry went through a difficult period. Working as individual farmers, growers had high expenses for fertilizer and packing materials and could not always meet the needs of multiple buyers. Finally, the farmers formed a cooperative association established with the help of Wilfrid Wheeler, then Secretary of the State Board of Agriculture. In 1922 there were 98 members in the Cape Cod Strawberry Growers Association. By pooling their orders for fertilizer and crates and selling to just one buying organization, they did better economically. In 1921 Falmouth shipped over 500,000 quarts of strawberries, excluding those sold locally. The berries would leave Falmouth at 9:00 PM and arrive in the Boston market at 6:00 AM.

Strawberry Picking 1940. *Courtesy Falmouth Historical Society.*

Recipes

Strawberry Breakfast Bread

In a large bowl, mix together:
   2/3 cup sugar
   3 eggs
   1/2 cup vegetable oil
   1 teaspoon vanilla

Sift together, then add to above mixture:
   2 cups flour
   1 teaspoon baking soda
   1 teaspoon baking powder
   1/4 teaspoon salt

Stir in:
   1 cup strawberries, sliced

Pour batter into a prepared eight-inch square pan. Top with a mixture of 1 teaspoon cinnamon, 2 teaspoons sugar. Bake at 350 degrees F. for 40 minutes.

Beach Plums

*This tasty fruit is one of the jewels of Cape Cod. Preserving the
fruit during the late summer is one of the joys of simple living.*
—*Cape Cod Cooperative Extension Fact Sheet*

Wild beach plums growing by
dunes at Sandy Neck Beach, East
Sandwich. *Courtesy Richard Uva;
www.beachplum.cornell.edu.*

Early each fall, a favorite pastime of Cape Codders is traveling along back
roads near the ocean to pick a tangy, deep purple fruit. The beach plum is
highly prized for making jams, sauces, muffins and even flavoring brandy.
New World explorers chronicled beach plums among the first plants they
saw in North America. In 1875, Samuel Adams Drake wrote of crossing a
range of sand hills in Truro where "beach plum, whortleberry, laurel, and
rhododendron grew wild." Attempts to grow beach plums on a commercial
scale have proved difficult since the annual yield is unpredictable. A bush
may be loaded with fruit one year and bare the next. Weather conditions at
the time the star-shaped white flowers blossom in May and June is thought
to be a critical factor. Heavy rain or frost can destroy blossoms or interfere
with pollination by bees.

In 1948 a group of 50 beach plum fans met in the Brewster Town Hall
and established the Cape Cod Beach Plum Grower's Association. They
studied techniques of propagation and sought methods of creating superior
beach plum jellies and jams. The edible fruit has a tart acidic taste. It varies
from one-half to one inch in diameter, and in color from red to deep blue to
purple. There are many opinions about the best way to prepare the highly
prized beach plum jam. The modern way is to add commercial pectin to
boiled fruit to make it thick. Traditionalists claim adding a small amount of
unripe beach plums (which contain high amounts of pectin) works better.
No matter what the recipe, this Cape Cod delicacy is a treat to enjoy with
morning toast or muffins.

Beach plums growing on author's property.

Recipes

Beach Plum Preserves

2 cups pitted beach plums (ripe and slightly unripe fruit)
1 to 1-1/2 cups sugar to taste

Place ingredients in a saucepan and bring to a boil. Reduce the heat to a very slow boil, stirring constantly. The mixture will be watery at first. Keep at low boil for about 30 minutes, with frequent stirring as it thickens. When you can pull the spoon along the bottom of the pan and the preserves separate allowing you to see the metal, cooking is complete. Pour into clean jars and keep refrigerated. Preserves will thicken when cooled. Yield: Two 6-oz. jars of preserves.

Beach Plum Brandy

2 cups beach plums, rinsed and drained
1 cup sugar
1 liter brandy

Put all ingredients into a large glass bottle or jar. Cover and place in a cool place. Let it sit for two weeks, swirling once a day to mix. After two weeks you are ready to decant into a clean bottle. Do not swirl, but gently pour through a sieve or filter into a clean container.

Note: This makes a lovely holiday gift packaged along with two liquor glasses easily found in an antique or thrift shop.

Scones with beach plum preserves

Turnips

Four-pound Eastham turnip with author's full grown cat, Rosebud.

The turnip is a root crop and has been used as a vegetable for human consumption in Europe since prehistoric times.
—www.hort.purdue.edu/newcrop/afcm/turnip

In the 18th century, Eastham was one of the most prominent farming communities on the Cape. Lacking good harbors, it depended more on agriculture than maritime trades. Its cranberries and asparagus were coveted on the Boston Market and grain production was plentiful enough to export to other localities. Another crop that did well in the sandy soil, and is celebrated to this day, is the Eastham turnip. Planted after the fourth of July, and harvested in November, those who taste them say they are unlike any others. Larger than the average purple and yellow turnip which are strong on the palate, Eastham turnips have a sweet mild taste. They are white in color with a purple top and approach the size of a softball.

Thoreau was so impressed with them that they were one of the four crops he planted in his garden along with peas, beans, and potatoes. Each November the Friends of the Eastham Library hold their Turnip Festival, usually on the Saturday before Thanksgiving. Activities include turnip bowling, contests for the biggest turnip, and a Mr. Turnip Head contest. There is a cooking contest and the Friends have published a cookbook, "First Encounter with a Turnip," that takes their prized crop to another level of creative cooking. My favorite way to prepare this delicious root vegetable is very simple and allows its sweet flavor to come through.

Turnips Lightly Coated with Bread Crumbs

1 pound Eastham turnips, peeled and cubed
3 tablespoons butter
4 tablespoons breadcrumbs
3 teaspoons minced parsley
Salt and pepper to taste

Steam turnips until tender, about 25-30 minutes. Remove from heat. Melt butter in a large frying pan. Add breadcrumbs and parsley. Add turnips and gently coat them with the crumbs, allowing mixture to heat through. Serve immediately.

Blueberries

Blueberries are one of the few truly blue foods on earth.
—*U.S. Highbush Blueberry Council*

Native Americans gathered blueberries from uplands and forests for centuries prior to the arrival of the colonists. They ate them fresh, used them for medicinal purposes and brewed strong teas to ease childbirth. The blossom end of each berry, with its perfect five-pointed star, was the basis of the belief that the Great Spirit sent the "star berry" to relieve children's hunger during time of famine. When the English settlers arrived, they found the low-growing wild blueberry similar to their whortleberry. The Wampanoags taught the colonists how to dry the berries under the sun and store them for winter use. One of the earliest recipes adapted from the native Wampanoags was for a dish called "samp." The following recipe gives an idea of what it may have tasted like.

Samp (Corn Pudding with Blueberries)

4 cups water
1/2 teaspoon salt
2 tablespoons butter
1-1/2 cups coarse ground corn meal
3/4 cup fresh blueberries

Bring water to boil in a large pot. Add the salt, butter and cornmeal, stirring until it returns to a boil. Turn the heat to low and cook gently for 20 minutes, stirring frequently. Remove from heat and let stand for one hour. Stir in blueberries and reheat over low heat. Water may be added if pudding is too thick.

Grandma Hayward's Blueberry Cake
(Written as it appeared in *What We Cook on Cape Cod*, published in 1911.) *Courtesy of Ned Handy, son of Amy Handy, Editor*

One well-beaten egg, add one cup of sugar and one tablespoonful of butter, melted, beat well and add one cup of milk and four cups of pastry flour sifted with three teaspoonfuls of baking powder. [Add] two cups of floured berries. Just before putting [it] in the oven sprinkle with sugar. Bake at 350 for 40 minutes.

Recipes

Rose Hips

*But sweet was the slight and spicy smell it
breathed from its heart invisible.*
—Emily Bronte, A Little Budding Rose

A sweet fragrance carried by sea breezes tells the Cape visitor that beach roses are nearby. More formally known as *Rosa rugosa*, this stunning flower, with hundreds of beautiful pink blooms, grows naturally all over Cape Cod. The plants however, with origins in Japan and China, are not native to the Cape. Although no one is sure, it's thought they might have been brought by English colonists in the 18th century. Early settlers used rose hip preparations to treat colds, urinary disorders and diarrhea. Ranging in color from yellow-orange to a rich crimson or purple, the rose hip is one of nature's highest sources of vitamin C and is rich in antioxidants.

Rosa rugosa plants are found in all types of habitats – pond edges, swamps, and, most prominently, open scrub areas by the beach. After the bloom dies, the berry-like seed pod or rose hip develops. Rose hips should be picked when they are bright red and slightly soft. They are generally cooked prior to eating, favored locally for tea or jam. They can be used fresh or dried. To dry them, spread fruit on a clean surface. Allow them to dry until the skin seems slightly shriveled. Split the hips and remove the seeds and hairs in the center. Let the hips dry completely. Freeze or store in sealed plastic bags. The following tea has a mild, but tangy flavor and is an astonishing beautiful pale pink.

Beach rose blossom and rose hips growing on bushes along Sandy Neck Beach in East Sandwich.

Rose Hip Tea

Place 6 rose hips into a non-aluminum* pan. Add two cups of water and bring to a boil. Simmer for 30 minutes. Strain and sweeten to taste.

*Aluminum destroys some of the vitamin C.

Wild Grapes

...the table was loaded with native fruits like plums, melons, grapes, and cranberries...
—Joanne Camas, *The First Thanksgiving.*

Cape Codders know when fall arrives by the delectable aroma of wild grapes growing on the twisted vines covering backyard fences and shrubs. Although one legend has it that Martha's Vineyard was named for this succulent purple fruit, there is no shortage of them on Cape Cod. Indeed, they can be found creeping along almost every side road or thicket exuding a fragrance that permeates the air. Along with their fruity aroma, wild grapes are distinguished by a deep purple color and watery flesh with a skin that slips off easily. Unlike the large compact bunches of cultivated grapes, those growing wild are scattered in smaller clusters.

Grape jelly is one of the all-time favorites produced by the century-old Green Briar Jam Kitchen in the Cape Cod town of East Sandwich. So plentiful are wild grapes that the jam kitchen does not have to purchase any; they get all they can use from generous local residents. Boston-born Ephraim W. Bull developed the famous Concord grape in 1849 from seeds of this native species. The Concord Grape Association web page indicates "he planted some 22,000 seedlings in all, before he had produced the ideal grape." The following recipe is an easy way to make grape juice.

Wild grapes growing on author's property.

Natural Grape Juice

2 cups wild or Concord grapes, rinsed and stems removed
6 cups of water

Place grapes in large saucepan. With a large spoon, mash grapes slightly Add water and bring to a boil. Reduce heat and simmer for 30 minutes. Place pot in refrigerator and let grapes sit in water overnight. Pour through sieve into serving pitcher. Add sugar or artificial sweetener to taste.

Native Indians made a dessert by boiling wild grapes, mashing them, and then adding cornmeal to the juice. Here's a similar recipe to show how it might have tasted.

Wild Grape Dumplings

1 cup flour
1-1/2 teaspoons baking powder
3 tablespoons sugar
1/4 teaspoon salt
1 tablespoon cooking oil
1/2 cup grape juice

Additional grape juice for boiling.

In a medium bowl, combine the first four ingredients. Add oil and grape juice and mix into a stiff dough. On a floured surface, roll dough very thin. Cut into 1/2-inch strips. Drop into boiling grape juice and cook for 15 minutes or until tender. Serve hot.

Note: You can use store-bought grape juice. Wild grape juice needs to be sweetened.

Chatham Fishing Boats, 2008, oil on panel, 9 x 12.

CHAPTER FIVE
HARVESTING THE SEA

We took great store of Cod-fish, for which we altered the name…
and called it Cape Cod.
—Gabriel Archer, 1602

Introduction

Almost two decades prior to the landing of the Mayflower, Bartholomew Gosnold and his crew, explored the waters around Cape Cod. They caught so many cod fish his chronicler, John Brereton, wrote:

…that we threw numbers of them overboard again: and surely, I am persuaded that in the months of March, April, and May, there is upon this coast, better fishing, and in as great plenty, as in Newfoundland: for the sculls of mackerel, herrings, cod, and other fish, that we daily saw as we went and came from the shore, were wonderful.

Many decades would pass, however, before Cape settlers reaped the bounty of the ocean. Farmers by tradition, they needed to first till the earth and carve out farms for basic survival. There were a few exceptions, though. The herring, or alewives, returned like clockwork to Cape ponds and brooks each spring. According to author Marise Fawsett, they "ran as thick as snowflakes in a blizzard." Taught by the native Indians how to gather them, the colonists made good use of alewives for food and fertilizer for cornfields. They would also catch fish and eels, or dig up clams for the dinner table, but fishing on a large scale did not take place until the colonists exhausted the land and crops diminished.

Brewster Fish Ladder, c.1950. *Courtesy Nickerson Archives, Cape Cod Community College.*

Drift whales stranded on Cape Cod Beach. c.1880 *Courtesy Nickerson Archives, Cape Cod Community College.*

Another product of the sea that literally came to the early colonists were the drift whales that frequently beached on shore. Cape Codders quickly appreciated the profits to be made from whale oil and blubber. The early whales swimming close to shore were slow-moving and floated when killed. Even more remarkable was the fact that they appeared during the fall when farmers where free from tending the land. These characteristics made them ideal to harvest, thus the name "right" whale. In time, when the numbers of beached whales diminished, Cape Cod fishermen went after them in small boats. As the whales retreated to deep waters, larger boats were needed, requiring deeper ports than the Cape offered. Even though Provincetown had seventeen deep sea whaling vessels at its peak, eventually Nantucket and New Bedford would eclipse Cape Cod in whaling. It was here however, that the industry began and spread. Indeed, it was the Yarmouth captain, Ichabod Paddock, who was invited to Nantucket to teach the trade in 1694.

As the fertility of the land declined, colonists turned to the sea. At first fishermen made short trips into the bay and surrounding waters for cod. As population and demand from Boston and New York markets grew, Cape fishermen ventured further, even hundreds of miles into sea for their catch. As early as 1730 they were engaged in a "triangle trade" sailing to the Grand Banks off Newfoundland, where they filled their vessels with abundant cod. After salting their catch on local beaches they would take the dried fish to the West Indies and trade them for molasses and rum. These fish were sold at far greater profits than they could bring locally and towns such as Chatham, Harwich and Barnstable prospered. As the number and size of boats increased, interest turned to Provincetown and its large deep harbor, until then, too remote for settlement.

Things changed dramatically during the Revolutionary War when British ships blockaded the waters all along the Cape. Fishing vessels sitting idle at their moorings decayed and became unfit for sailing. After the war, in order to once again stimulate the fishing industry, Congress granted a bounty on all exported cod. The fleets quickly rebounded and Provincetown took the lead. By 1802 it had 33 vessels that regularly sailed to the Grand Banks for cod. Half of the catch was salted on Labrador beaches, half at home. In Provincetown, fish were brought to shore in dories, washed clean of sea salt and carried up to "flakes" in wheelbarrows. Flakes were low slatted platforms on which the washed, split and resalted fish were laid to dry in the sun. In the years following the War of 1812, almost every town on the Cape had fleets of fishing vessels going after Grand Banks cod and mackerel.

Drying Fish in Provincetown. c.1890 *Courtesy Nickerson Archives, Cape Cod Community College.*

Provincetown Fishing Fleet, c.1912.
Courtesy Nickerson Archives, Cape Cod Community College.

Salt was needed in vast quantities to preserve cod and mackerel heading for distant markets. Until 1776, the colonists used the European method of boiling sea water in open pans until it evaporated leaving a residue of salt. The process was slow, used enormous quantities of wood, and produced very little salt. In *The Saltworks of Cape Cod*, William Quinn points out, "It took almost two cords of firewood to boil down four hundred gallons of sea water and produce one bushel of salt." As Cape forests became denuded, fuel for boiling became scarce and led to a shortage of salt. Compounding this, during the War for Independence, English blockades stopped all salt imports. In the late 1700s, Captain John Sears of East Dennis realized the Atlantic Ocean could be a veritable gold mine when it came to extracting salt. He decided to try a new way to extract salt from seawater – evaporation by sunlight. He built simple troughs of soft white pine, approximately 10 feet wide by 50 feet long by 10 feet deep. The vats were crude, leaked and it took prodigious work to carry buckets of sea water to fill them. These initial attempts were derided as "Sears Folly," but he persisted. Major Nathaniel Freeman of Harwich sug-

gested the use of windmills to pump the sea water, easing the burden. In 1793 Reuben Sears of Harwich invented a movable roof on wooden rails that could be quickly rolled over the vats to protect the process from rain.

Saltworks then surged on Cape Cod. By 1802 there were 136 salt-making establishments. The war of 1812 further increased the industry. When President Thomas Jefferson ordered an embargo against foreign trade, the price of salt skyrocketed to eight dollars a bushel. Between 1810 and 1831 the capacity of the Cape's saltworks increased 300 percent. In peak years of the 1830s there were 881 saltworks with an output of a quarter million bushels of salt annually. Hundreds of canvas-sailed windmills pumped seawater into this vast network of vats. By the 1840s, when fishing in New England declined and the railroad brought in lower cost mined salt from other parts of the country, the salt works began to disappear. In 1865 there were only three active salt works left. Cape Codders, known to be resourceful, recognized that salt-preserved wood from the abandoned vats was especially good for building, so it was used for home construction. Many of those homes still dot the Cape today.

Saltworks, South Yarmouth, c.1900. The sea water went through three stages or "rooms." First, was evaporation and precipitation of plant life; then the "pickle" room with the precipitation of lime; finally the "salt room" where the product crystallized. *Courtesy Sturgis Library Archives, Barnstable, MA.*

The majority of Cape fishermen could not afford the large ships that took others into deep water. Until the trawl line was introduced in 1858, cod were caught by hand line from dories with clams or squid as bait. Most had small boats. Since they were no match for a storm at sea, they fished close to shore. They would bring lightly salted "fresh" fish home for local use or to sell in the Boston Market. Meanwhile, other areas of the Cape developed their maritime activities. Wellfleet fishermen caught mackerel and oysters, Chatham had twenty-five vessels that sailed to the distant Grand Banks and the area between Nantucket and Nova Scotia. A major event in the growth of the Cape's fishing industry came with the opening of Georges Bank in 1821. Little more than a day's sail from the Cape, Henry Kittredge wrote, "this discovery meant as much as striking oil in his cattle range means to a ranch-owner." The nearer source of cod and halibut brought quick riches to not only Provincetown fishermen, but those in Chatham, Harwich and Dennis as well. Wellfleet specialized in mackerel-catching and had a fleet of a hundred vessels.

In 1853, the "purse" seine was developed replacing the more tedious line fishing. It made it possible to catch huge schools of mackerel and business boomed. Although Cape fishermen led the way, Marise Fawsett writes in *Cape Cod Annals*, "when big business entered the race, and size became the dominant factor – big investment, big vessels, and big harbors – competition narrowed accordingly," and Cape fishermen could not compete. Although the Civil War disrupted much of the Cape's fishing business, it actually opened up more markets for Provincetown's fishermen. Portuguese sailors suffering from lack of work in their homelands were happy to find employment when American ships in the Azores and Cape Verde Islands offered jobs. Scores came to work and live in Provincetown. In 1875, there were 25 coastal and 36 ocean vessels operating in that town, more than in any community of the state including Boston. Provincetown was a bustling place with all the ancillary maritime businesses such as ship chandlers, shipwrights, sail makers, caulkers, riggers, and blacksmiths.

Provincetown Fishermen Casting Nets, c.1912. *Courtesy Nickerson Archives, Cape Cod Community College.*

Deck of a quahog digger, c.1921. *Courtesy Nantucket Athenaeum.*

Chatham and Provincetown are still able to support a small commercial fishing fleet. Shell fishing for oysters, quahogs, soft-shelled clams, bay scallops, and sea clams are still an important part of Wellfleet's economy. At one time, Wellfleet shell-fishermen would import seed oysters from Buzzards Bay, Connecticut, and the Chesapeake to plant them in the harbor to absorb the famous Wellfleet flavor. When full grown, they re-harvested them for the Boston Market. As the production of native oysters gradually increased this practice was no longer necessary. Salty and crisp with a mild finish, Wellfleet oysters are known around the world for their unique flavor. Recreational shell fishing is now a traditional Cape and Islands pastime. Each town has its own regulations and a permit is required.

Chatham fishermen unloading cod, 2008.

Bins of cod destined for market after unloading.

Clams 101:

Hard-shelled or Quahog clams

Hard clams or quahogs are buried in the intertidal zone and can be found in depths up to 50 feet. Quahogs are sold under three categories according to size: *Chowders* are the largest variety and they can be three inches or more in size. Since they tend to be tough, they are used in chowders, stuffed clams and fritters. *Cherrystones* are medium-sized. They are less chewy and are commonly used in pasta dishes or in the traditional clambake. *Littlenecks* are the smallest and can be eaten raw or steamed in clam broth.

Note: Quahog shells were the traditional shells from which the native Indians made wampum. Their scientific name, *Mercenaria mercenaria* is related to the Latin word for money.

Soft-shelled (*Mya arenaria*)

Soft-shelled clams or steamers, have thinner shells compared to quahogs. They are found in tidal mud flats about 6-10 inches below the surface. As filter feeders, they draw in water through a siphon and expel it after food particles are filtered out. Telltale holes that squirt water when pressure is applied around them are a clue that steamers are below. In addition to steaming, they may be fried or used in chowder.

Clamming on the Harwich flats.

Bucket of steamers, 2008.

75

Cape Cod Seafood Sampler

Recipes

Baked Stuffed Clams

Steamed Clams

3 pounds live clams in the shell.

These can be cherrystones, littlenecks or steamers. Prior to cooking, scrub clams and rinse in cold water to remove sand.

3 tablespoons butter
1 small onion, chopped
4 cloves garlic, chopped
1 liter dry white wine
6 stems of parsley
melted unsalted butter

In a large steamer pot melt the 3 tablespoons of butter and lightly sauté the onion and garlic. Add the wine and bring to slow boil. Add clams and parsley and cover pot. Steam just until clams open, about 6-10 minutes. Do not overcook and keep an eye on the pot so the liquid doesn't boil over. Discard any clams that do not open. Serve with melted unsalted butter or clam broth. Serves 2-3 people.

Baked Stuffed Clams

1 dozen littleneck or cherrystone clams.

Steam clams and remove from shells. Finely chop clams and set aside. Save shells for stuffing.

3 tablespoons butter
1/2 small onion, finely diced
1 clove garlic, finely minced
1/2 small red pepper, finely diced
1 small stalk celery, finely minced
1/3 cup cracker crumbs
1 tablespoon fresh parsley, finely minced
paprika to taste
Parmesan cheese to taste

Melt butter in medium pan. Add next four ingredients. Cook mixture until soft. Add cracker crumbs, parsley and clams. Mix well. Fill shells with a tablespoon of filling and sprinkle with paprika and Parmesan cheese. Bake at 400 degrees F. for 8 minutes. Serve immediately. Makes 3 appetizer servings.

Note: Fresh clams may be replaced with a 6-1/2 oz. can of minced clams, drained.

Cape Cod Clam Chowder (From *What We Cook on Cape Cod ~ 1911*)

One quart of clams thoroughly cleaned, one quart of milk, one good sized onion, six potatoes, four slices of pork, one tablespoon of butter, three crackers, broken, pepper. Fry out the pork and then put in the sliced onion and cook a few minutes; put them into a large kettle and add the sliced potatoes; boil them till soft in water to cover them; add the clam water (after straining), then the clams. Cook five minutes, then add the quart of milk, and when it comes to a boil add butter, cracker and pepper. Enough for six or eight persons.

Cornmeal Coated Striped Bass with Warm Cranberry Compote

Warm Cranberry Compote
    1-1/2 cups dried sweetened cranberries
    zest and juice of 2 medium oranges
    zest and juice of 2 medium lemons
    1/2 cup sugar
    1 teaspoon vanilla
    1 tablespoon corn starch mixed in 2 tablespoons water

Cover cranberries with very warm water and let sit 10 minutes. Place cranberries with the water in a small sauce pan. Add orange and lemon zest, juices, and sugar. Bring to a simmer and cook for 10-15 minutes to reduce slightly. Stir frequently. Add 1 teaspoon vanilla and the cornstarch mixture. Cook further just until thickened. Keep warm.

Note: Dried cranberries have an advantage over fresh since they are available all year as well as keeping a nice round form and not bursting during cooking.

Cornmeal Coated Striped Bass
    3 pounds skinless filets of striped bass
    1 cup flour
    3 eggs mixed in bowl with a little water
    1 cup cornmeal
    1/4 cup canola oil

Cut bass on the bias into 1/4 pound medallions. Dredge fish in flour, egg wash, and then cornmeal. Heat the oil in a large frying pan. Place fish in pan and cook for 4 minutes on each side until golden. Serves six.

Cornmeal Coated Striped Bass with Warm Cranberry Compote

Golden Scallops with Pineapple-Ginger Sauce

Pineapple Ginger Sauce
   1 cup crushed pineapple in juice
   1 tablespoons corn starch
   1/2 teaspoon fresh grated ginger
   dash of garlic powder
   1/4 cup vinegar
   1/2 cup brown sugar
   2 tablespoons soy sauce

   Mix the pineapple and cornstarch in a small sauce pan. Heat on medium heat until thickened. Add the remaining ingredients, stirring to mix well. Cook for several minutes to heat through. Keep warm.

Golden Scallops
   1-1/2 pounds sea scallops
   1/4 cup flour
   3 tablespoons cooking oil

   Coat scallops on flat side with flour. Heat oil in a large frying pan (cast iron preferred). Add prepared scallops and cook for two minutes on each side or until golden. Serve immediately with a side dish of the pineapple-ginger sauce. Serves 4.

Golden Scallops with Pineapple-Ginger Sauce

Traditional Provincetown Kale Soup

There are many ways to cook this Portuguese specialty. This is a basic recipe to which other vegetables such as tomatoes or summer squash may be added.

2 tablespoons olive oil
1 large onion, chopped
1 pound linguiça sausage, sliced
6 cups chicken broth
1 pound kale, broken in pieces
2 cups potatoes, cubed
1 tablespoon vinegar
1/2 teaspoon salt (optional)
pepper to taste
1 (15-ounce) can white kidney beans

Heat the oil in a large pot. Sauté the onion and linguiça for 5 minutes, stirring occasionally. Add the chicken broth and bring to a boil. Add the kale, potatoes, vinegar, salt and pepper. Bring to a second boil and lower heat to a simmer. Cook until potatoes are tender, about 30 minutes. Add the beans and simmer for an additional five minutes. Serves 6.

Oyster Stew

4 tablespoons butter
1 cup celery, finely chopped
24 oysters, shelled, with liquid
4 cups milk, hot
1 teaspoon Worcestershire sauce
salt and pepper to taste
paprika

Sauté celery in butter until tender. Add oysters with their juice. Heat just until oysters begin to curl. Add milk. Bring to a simmer. Do not boil. Add Worcestershire sauce and salt and pepper to taste. Garnish with paprika for color. Serves 4.

Cod Poached in Spicy Tomato Sauce

1 tablespoon olive oil
2 cloves garlic, chopped
1 small onion, chopped
1 small green pepper, chopped
1 (14-ounce) can stewed tomatoes with basil and oregano
3/4 teaspoon crushed red pepper
1 teaspoon chili power
1-1/2 pounds cod fish cut in 4 filets

Heat the olive oil in a large nonstick skillet over medium-high heat. Add garlic, onion, and green pepper and sauté for 1-2 minutes. Add the stewed tomatoes, red pepper and chili powder. Bring to simmer. Add fish, cover and cook on medium heat for 8-10 minutes or until fish flakes easily when tested with a fork. Serves 4.

Cod Poached in Spicy Tomato Sauce

Lobster Bisque

Lobster Bisque

1 cup cooked lobster meat in small pieces, set aside
3 tablespoons butter
1 small onion, chopped
1 stalk celery, chopped
2 tablespoons flour
2 cups milk
2 tablespoons tomato paste
1/2 teaspoon curry powder

Sauté the onion and celery in butter until soft. Add flour to make a roux, then add milk. Stir to make a creamy consistency. While stirring, add tomato paste and curry power. Add lobster meat and heat thoroughly but do not boil. Serve immediately. Serves 4.

Model of a Packet Ship. *Courtesy Nickerson Archives, Cape Cod Community College.*

Schooner *Bloomer* in Barnstable Harbor, c.1900. *Courtesy Sturgis Library Archives, Barnstable, MA.*

Schooner *Bloomer* in Barnstable Harbor, c.1900. *Courtesy Sturgis Library Archives, Barnstable, MA.*

CHAPTER SIX
SHIPS AND SHIPMASTERS

Those venerable retired captains who, in their advancing years, still remain in almost every Cape town, constitute one of the most substantial elements of the population.
—Simeon Deyo ed., *History of Barnstable County, Massachusetts*

After the War of 1812 cod and mackerel fishing not only picked up again, but flourished as boat building resumed. Salt manufacturing skyrocketed and quickly surpassed the needs of local fishermen. There was a ready market not only for salt, but other Cape products like onions, flax, and wood, if only there was a way to get it to Boston. At the same time, passengers were getting tired of undependable, uncomfortable journeys by stage coach. Enter the Cape Cod packet ships. Although it was possible prior to this time to ship goods or carry the occasional passenger to Boston from the Cape, packet ships were the first commercial vessels to do so with any regularity. These moderately sized vessels, built with local timber by Cape Cod men became the principal means of carrying mail, cargo, and passengers from Cape Cod to Boston or New York during the first decades of the 1800s. Kittredge writes in *Cape Cod: Its People and Their History*, "These craft were as complete and absolute products of the region as anything made by man can be." Just about every Cape village had two or three packets that made weekly trips to Boston. Competition was fierce among the towns to have the best outfitted, most comfortable, and fastest ship. The boats held from twenty-five to fifty passengers of all classes. On board, passengers might be entertained by the tales of an old seaman regaling his experience outwitting pirates on the China seas. The round trip ticket from Cape Cod to Boston was $1.50 and meals were twenty-five cents.

Quite often, an arriving packet would carry a shipmaster coming home via Boston. Having docked his larger ship in that deeper port, he might be returning to the Cape after a 16- to 18-month voyage from China. When a packet was sighted in the northern part of Yarmouth, signal poles on high points would fly coats or flags to alert south shore residents. One can easily imagine the excitement of family members greatly anticipating the return of their beloved patriarch. Author Henry David Thoreau, who traveled through the area by stage coach, took a lesser view of the scene. In his book, *Cape Cod*, he wrote, "It appeared as if this use must absorb the greater part of the old clothes of the Cape, leaving but few rags for the peddlers."

Significant not only for carrying passengers and goods, the packets (and later, the coastal schooners) brought about the development of allied trades and work on shore: blacksmith shops, ship's carpenters, sail lofts, and ship chandlers. These smaller ships kept shopkeepers well supplied and, importantly, were training grounds for Cape Cod men who would graduate to the international packet trade and foreign ports.

Ultimately it would be those who honed their skills on the Cape Cod packet ships who were chosen to command the majestic clipper ships. These vessels with their tapering concave bows, towering masts, and square sails were the finest and fastest sailing ships ever known. The Cape did not have deep harbors to accommodate these massive vessels which ruled the seas in the mid 1800s, but its sons were behind the wheels, many setting records that still stand.

Clipper Ship *Chariot of Fame. Courtesy Historical Society of Old Yarmouth, MA.*

Captain Asa Eldridge

Captain Asa Eldridge. *Courtesy Historical Society of Old Yarmouth, MA.*

...throwing the Red Jacket into the wind, helm hard down, he backed her long side of the berth without aid, while the crew took in sail with a celerity that seemed like magic to the spectators – a superb piece of seamanship.
—Yarmouth Register

On January 11, 1854, Yarmouth born Asa Eldridge took the helm of the clipper *Red Jacket* for its maiden voyage from New York to Liverpool. Sailing the north Atlantic through winter gales with "snow, hail, or rain every day," he arrived in Liverpool in 13 days and 1 hour. At a time when there was fierce competition for speed, alerted crowds of thousands lined the shore to see his arrival. This record for a sailing ship is still unsurpassed. Magnifying his fame further he charged into port passing the tug boats ready to tow him into the harbor. As described in the January 23, 1854 edition of the *Yarmouth Register*:

> Then Captain Asa Eldridge gave them a thrill they least expected – he took in his kites, his skysails, royals and topgallants, hung his courses or lower sails, in their gear, ignored the tugs that caught up, and, throwing the Red Jacket into the wind, helm hard down, he backed her long side of the berth without aid, while the crew took in sail with a celerity that seemed like magic to the spectators – a superb piece of seamanship.

While we might imagine a shipmaster of old having a life of adventure and exotic travel, the challenges he needed to overcome were tremendous. Among his responsibilities were provisioning his boat, selecting a crew, acting as agent in procuring cargo, charting the course, and managing customs documents. Most of his skill however, came forward when he had to deal with the unforeseen: violent storms, mutinous or deserting crewmen, besetting calms, or devious foreign traders. Whatever hardship he faced, he needed to maintain a sharp, resourceful mind and strong character. In those early days, the sea captains were our country's primary ambassadors.

The extraordinary experiences of Captain Elijah Cobb of Brewster were preserved in his journal. Cobb, a young man of 26, had already made two voyages to Europe as first mate, and was in command of the ship *Jane*, bound for Cadiz, Spain. It was 1794 during Robespierre's "Bloody Reign of Terror" when a French frigate captured his ship off Brest, France. Desperate, Cobb later wrote, "All my papers had been taken from me. My vessel was there, but her cargo, flour and rice, was taken out and was daily made into bread, soups, etc., for the half-starved populace, and without papers I could not even substantiate my claim to an empty ship." Impatient while enduring weeks of delay, he wrote to the American *charge des affaires* in Paris. He was told to be patient and "the government would do what was right in time." Honoring their word and decreeing his ship a neutral vessel, he was notified he would be paid for the stolen cargo. Unfortunately, since money could not be taken out of France, he settled upon taking bills of exchange that could be redeemed by the French agent in Hamburg, Germany. After waiting a month and never receiving the bills, he sent his crew home aboard ship and decided to take his case to Paris headquarters.

Aware of the mass slaughter of people during this time, Cobb made the three day journey with much anxiety, later writing, "I did not get one wink during the journey of 684 miles" and he took only an occasional mouthful of bread washed down with "low priced red Burgundy wine." Upon arrival in Paris, he was told there were no documents supporting his claim. As he was trying to decide what to do, he later wrote in his journal... "a French gentleman, who occupied the next room, [in the Hotel de Boston] passed my door. I asked him in and related to him my grievances. He advised me to endeavor to obtain an interview with Robespierre, assuring me he was partial to Americans." Cobb did so, and to his relief the interview was granted. After their meeting, Robespierre wrote a letter to the authorities indicating if the papers were not produced immediately they would "hear from me again in a way not so pleasing." Cobb was given his papers, reached Hamburg and secured his payment ...a day before the bills expired.

Captain Elijah Cobb of Brewster. From a French pastel, 1794. *Courtesy Brewster Ladies Library.*

Although filled with adventure and exotic travel, life on the sea was monotonous, lonely, and dangerous. It took skill and bravery to bring a ship successfully to port, particularly under adverse conditions. Captain Allen H. Knowles of Yarmouth successfully sailed the clipper ship, *Chariot of Fame*, from Liverpool to Provincetown in January 1854. Mid-Atlantic winter gales caused the topsail to be blown loose and broke the main yard. High seas flooded the cabin and carried away four small boats on board. Relentless, the sea blew additional sails from their gaskets and carried away the figurehead. A final blinding snowstorm assaulted the boat before it finally arrived, broken but steadfast in Provincetown Harbor.

An even more harrowing journey on *Chariot of Fame* occurred after he set sail from New York bound for Acapulco with a cargo of coal. His ship's log states:

Monday, August 18, 1856. Have had violent gales and a high dangerous sea the last three days. Saturday morning, the fourth mate in irons for threatening desperate vengeance on me for reprimanding him for neglect of duty.

Sunday, August 24: All hands employed securing the coal. Ship has got a 4 streak list. What hard luck I do have.

Monday, August 25: Very thick snow storm; a heavy sea from the west.

Wednesday, August 27: This is the longest and hardest passage I ever had round Cape Horn; in fact it has been a very tedious passage throughout. Barcella Polena fell from the fore top to the deck; killed himself instantly. My crew are getting pretty well bunged up, and I am getting well tired of this weather.

Monday, September 8: This is the first time for thirty days we have had all sail set.

Thursday, September 11: Ends with hard gales from W.N.W. and very squally. In God's name when shall I get a fair wind. Over forty days since we have had one.

In the end, after one hundred and forty-five days at sea, the voyage finally ended at Acapulco.

Captain Alan Hinkley Knowles. *Courtesy Historical Society of Old Yarmouth, MA.*

Edward Penniman of Eastham was one of the most successful sea captains in New England. Beginning his career on the sea at age 11 years, he worked as cook's helper on a schooner bound for the Grand Banks. He embarked on his first whaling expedition when he was 21 years old. Soon after, he became a captain of his own ship and established his base in New Bedford. Although his letters home mention the trials and hardships he faced on the sea and the sentiment that he preferred life on land, it was hard to resist the wealth he knew he would gain. A tally listed in Deyo's *History of Barnstable County, Massachusetts* indicates: "on various voyages, he took 4,237 barrels of sperm oil, 12,096 barrels of whale oil and 166,871 pounds of whale bone." The going rate for whale oil in the 1860's varied from $1.50 to $2.50 a gallon. Whale-bone brought over $15 per pound – very profitable indeed. Another incentive for Captain Penniman's long voyages was exposure to foreign cultures which fascinated him.

Captain Edward Penniman, taken in his parlor prior to 1913.
Courtesy National Park Service, Cape Cod National Sea Shore.

Captain Penniman House. 2006, oil on canvas, 11 x 14.

In 1884, at age fifty-three, Captain Penniman had enough sailing. He joined his family in the French Second Empire home in the Fort Hill section of Eastham which he built in 1868. No expense had been spared in creating this elegant mansion overlooking Nauset Marsh and the more distant Atlantic.

In addition to elegant architectural detailing, ornate interior woodwork and superb craftsmanship, it was the first house in Eastham to have indoor plumbing. The house is preserved and now managed by the National Park Service. It is open for ranger-guided tours during the summer.

Portion of a letter from Captain Penniman to his son Ned (with original spelling and punctuation):

Oct. 29th 1882

It is almost calm, the sails are slap banging against the mast. I expect you have forgotten all about Ships by this time, & I hope you will never learn again. I hope you will not be a Sailor, at the best [it is a miserable] life to follow, full of hardships & trials, to say nothing about being away from home, & friends, for long years at a time, you must try to learn all you can at School, so by the time you are 20 years old I hope you will have a much better education than I did at that age, by & by when you become a man, & go out into the world you will see the need of it, this is the way I found it ...So good by,
All well. Love to all, Father.

No less remarkable than the captain was his wife, Augusta Knowles Penniman, who accompanied her husband on three of his voyages, each time taking along one or two of their three children. She was 26 years old on her first voyage with her husband and brought along their son Eugene, (Genia), who was just four years old. In contrast to her husband, her writings suggest she actually enjoyed life at sea, learning how to navigate and offering her cooking and sewing skills to help out. Many of her journal entries, from 1864 to 1868 on the whaling bark *Minerva*, reveal activities not unlike those she would have assumed on land:

Dec. 28, 1865: Been washing feel tired. Morning ironed, mended, afternoon I [done] chores.
Dec. 29: Cool, but head winds. Spent the day in sewing, reading and writing. All well. Extracted two of Genia under teeth.
July 3, 1867: A fine day. I spent it in sewing, reading and writing. At ten P.M. lowered the boats and took a nice fat whale. I call it a fourth of July whale.

As routine as most of the journey may have been, there were moments of splendor and excitement in the exotic places the Pennimans anchored. Augusta's journal entry of Dec. 3, 1865 written while in Hawaii reads:

Afternoon Edward & Capt. Jones got horses, and accompanied Mrs. J. and Rev. Mr. & Mrs. Damon with myself to the noted place called the Devil's Punch Bowl. It is a high mountain and in order to ascend it, it is necessary to ride horseback. Upon reaching its top, we have a full view of the city with all its valley residences, and [taru] patches, also a splendid view of the harbor and its shipping.

Out of devotion or desire for adventure there were other women who joined their husbands at sea. Mary Chipman Lawrence of Falmouth, along with their five year-old daughter Minnie, accompanied her husband, Captain Samuel Lawrence, as he set sail on a 108-foot whaling bark to the Pacific and Arctic Oceans. Monotony soon surpassed her early curiosity and excitement being at sea. An entry in her diary, later published as The *Captain's Best Mate: The Journal of Mary Chipman Lawrence on the Whaler Addison, 1856-1860*, reveals her loneliness at sea: "How much I have thought of loving friends today." But her strong sense of duty prevailed, "How ungrateful should I be to complain," she wrote, "it would be delightful indeed to see friends near and dear, but uninterrupted happiness is not for mortals to enjoy."

Captain Penniman's son Edward (Neddie) Penniman, *Courtesy National Park Service, Cape Cod National Sea Shore.*

On June 10, 1855 Hannah Rebecca Burgess, from the Town of Sandwich, was a young bride of twenty-one when she accompanied her husband Captain William Burgess on the extreme clipper ship *Challenger*. Hannah had sailed previously with her husband on the ship *Whirlwind*, and not only enjoyed it, but made good use of her time. In a journal entry on that earlier trip she wrote, "I am trying to get initiated into sea phrases." She studied Nathaniel Bowditch's *American Practical Navigator* and read Richard Dana's *Two Years Before the Mast*, an account of his seaman's voyage to California in the 1830s. Evidence of her pluck showed in a journal entry where she wrote of the violent weather encountered rounding Cape Horn on the *Whirlwind*: "I should like to have been on deck even though it meant being lashed to the rigging." After 18 months into his travels around the world on the *Challenger*, Captain Burgess and his crew had spent 51 days loading 1,600 tons of guano fertilizer in Callao, Peru. They were destined for Chile, when the illness he had been fighting for weeks became worse. After the ship left Peru, he quickly deteriorated and died. With 1,600 tons of fertilizer to deliver and a first mate considered incompetent, the 22-year old Hannah assumed charge and successfully brought the full-rigged clipper ship into Valparaiso.

Hannah Rebecca Burgess at 18 years. A daguerreotype taken in 1852, the year she became the bride of Capt. William Burgess. *Courtesy Sandwich Historical Society.*

In 1869 Donald McKay built the last of his great clipper ships, *Glory of the Seas*. Three Cape men in succession commanded her: Josiah Knowles of Eastham, Elisha F. Sears of Brewster, and Joshua Freemen, Jr., also from Brewster. The latter served as her captain for eighteen years. Today, an abundance of beautifully preserved sea captain homes remain all along the Cape. Centerville, Barnstable, and Brewster have large concentrations, as does the "Captain's Mile" in Yarmouth Port. The only Cape Cod captain's house that is open to the public on a regular basis is the *Bangs Hallet House* in Yarmouth Port, which is now home to the Historical Society of Old Yarmouth. The home was occupied by more than one shipmaster and visitors learn that one of these, Captain Allen Hinckley Knowles, famous as master of *Chariot of Fame*, did needlepoint to pass away his leisure time.

Captain Bangs Hallet House, Yarmouth Port, MA.

The full-rigged *Jason* was blown ashore in a fierce northeast wind and wrecked December 5, 1893. Twenty-five men died; one was rescued and survived. *Courtesy William P. Quinn and the U.S. Coast Guard Heritage Museum, Barnstable, MA.*

CHAPTER SEVEN
SAFEGUARDING THOSE AT SEA

When men are lost on the beach, the whole Cape takes it very much to heart,
talks about it, mulls over it; when men are saved, there is no place where they
are treated with greater hospitality and kindness.
—Henry Beston, *The Outermost House: A Year of Life on the Great Beach of Cape Cod*

Ship Kate Harding ashore, Truro,
1892. *Courtesy National Park Service,*
Cape Cod National Sea Shore.

From the earliest periods of exploration and shipping, the waters surrounding Cape Cod and the Islands were a mariner's nightmare. Thought to be the most dangerous winter coast in the world, sand bars extending far into sea, deceivingly shallow water over shoals, treacherous storms, and heavy fog resulted in thousands of shipwrecks. Yet, the sea was the essential highway for merchant trade, foreign commerce, and New Englanders who fished as a livelihood.

Earliest efforts to save lives from shipwrecks came about when Congress established the Massachusetts Humane Society in 1786. This society, mostly volunteers, erected crude huts along Nauset Beach, Race Point, and Chatham to shelter survivors of shipwrecks who would otherwise perish from exposure on the isolated beaches. The huts were equipped with blankets, firewood, and food. Later, small boats and rope lines were added for volunteer crews on shore to help those stranded. Although a benevolent action, the huts did little to save lives of the many sailors who did not make it to land. Often, Cape residents stood helplessly on shore as men froze on their ships or were washed overboard.

Halfway House on Cape Cod, now at Mystic Seaport, CT.
Courtesy National Park Service, Cape Cod National Sea Shore.

Lighthouses

Lighthouses, from ancient times, have fascinated members of the human race.
There is something about a lighted beacon that suggests hope and trust and appeals
to the better instincts of mankind.
—Edward Rowe Snow

A significant improvement to navigational safety was the erection of lighthouse stations along the outer coast. The first to be erected, Highland Light, was built in response to a letter to Congress in 1794 by the Reverend James Freeman who expressed deep concern over the great number of shipwrecks that occurred off the east coast of Truro. Consequently, the government purchased ten acres of land from Isaac Small in Truro for $110 and George Washington authorized the building of a 45-foot, wooden light station. Highland Light was erected in 1797 and stood five hundred feet from the edge of the bluff.

A little over a decade later after the single tower at Highland Light was established, the twin lighthouses in Chatham were built. In that early period, mariners identified the lighthouses by the number of lights rather than timed blinks, as they do now. Thus the Chatham Light Station had two wooden towers. When the light station at Nauset was built, there were three towers, known as the "three sisters." As more lighthouses were erected, this system became impractical and unique timed or sequenced signals were developed for each tower. With increasing maritime activities becoming a source of great profit to the country, Congress quickly voted funds to fully illuminate the coast. Race Point Light (1816) was the first of three lighthouses in Provincetown. It was followed by Long Point (1826) and Wood End (1872).

Romanticized by writers and poets, the life of the isolated lighthouse keeper was actually very lonely and dangerous. When a storm raged and others might head for a cozy hearth, the keeper had to be most attentive. At other times, long solitary hours would be spent in mundane tasks such as carrying heavy buckets of oil up dozens of stairs, filling oil lamps, cleaning reflectors, maintaining equipment and doing general housekeeping. In the early days of lighthouses whale oil was the source of fuel for illumination, but was very inefficient. Only three percent of the light could be seen from any distance at sea. The sooty coating it produced had to be constantly cleaned from the glass surrounding the lamp. At the beginning of the 19th century, lighting improved with the invention of the Argand lamp. This mechanism with a silvered metal reflector increased the amount of visible light by thirty-nine percent. The greatest improvement however, came with the Fresnel lens. In 1819 Augustin Fresnel of France used a series of prisms to bend and concentrate light focusing all the rays into one concentrated beam. Eighty percent of the light was now visible twenty miles at sea. Fresnel's system was immediately adopted throughout the world.

In the 1850s, author Henry David Thoreau, stayed at the Highland Light. In his book *Cape Cod*, he wrote of accompanying the keeper to the lantern:

> *He led the way first through his bedroom, which was placed nearest to the lighthouse, and then through a long, narrow, covered passageway, between whitewashed walls, like a prison-entry, into the lower part of the lighthouse, where many great butts of oil were arranged around; thence we ascended by a winding and open iron stairway, with a steadily increasing scent of oil and lamp-smoke, to*

Highland Light, Truro; c. 1912.
Courtesy Nickerson Archives,
Cape Cod Community College.

a trap-door in an iron floor, and through this into the lantern. It was a neat building, with everything in apple-pie order, and no danger of anything rusting there for want of oil. The light consisted of fifteen Argand lamps, placed within smooth concave reflectors twenty-one inches in diameter, and arranged in two horizontal circles one above the other, facing every way excepting directly down the Cape. These were surrounded, at a distance of two or three feet, by large plate-glass windows, which defied the storms, with iron sashes, on which rested the iron cap. All the iron work, except the floor, was painted white.

Thoreau, conversed with the keeper as he lighted each lamp in succession, "at the same moment that many a sailor on the deep witnessed the lighting of the Highland Light." Today there are fourteen lighthouses on the Cape. Some are in private hands or have been deactivated, but each has a rich legacy and many stories to tell. Following are just a few.

In the early 1800s, Barnstable Harbor was an active trading and fishing port. The first light station, built on the west side of the harbor in 1827, consisted of a wooden lantern on the roof of a keeper's house. Its fixed light welcomed Barnstable fishermen from nine miles out on Cape Cod Bay. It shone for three decades until replaced by the brick tower (painted white) that stands today. Although lighthouse keepers were for the most part men, many brave women undertook the role; usually after a husband or father died. In the winter of 1862, keeper Thomas Baxter was struggling to navigate his dory through the ice clogged waters of Barnstable Harbor when he badly injured his leg. After it became gangrenous and led to death, his wife Lucy took over his responsibilities. She was an able caretaker from 1862 to 1867 while raising her three children in the keeper's house.

Sandy Neck Light, 2007, oil on canvas, 9 x 12.

In 1829, the year Nobska Light Station was established, records indicate over 10,000 vessels passed through Vineyard Sound. The early 19th century Falmouth whaling fleet, as well as merchant vessels and schooners needed to be safely guided into Little Harbor and Great Harbor in Woods Hole. In addition, Falmouth was a major port for packet boats traveling between New York and Boston. Oliver A. Nickerson had the longest stay of any keeper in the station's history, from 1874 to 1911. One of the responsibilities was to count the number of vessels passing the light. From 1901 to 1908 his daughter, Florence Nickerson, was the official "observer" at the station.

Nobska Light, 2005, oil on canvas, 11 x 14.

Three Sisters Light Station. C.1890 *Courtesy Nickerson Archives, Cape Cod Community College.*

Winslow Lewis, the low-bidder who erected the original three fifteen-foot brick towers known to mariners as the "three sisters" was criticized for shoddy work. In 1892, as coastline erosion threatened their collapse, they were replaced by three wooden towers farther inland. Less than two decades later, they too were on the verge of toppling into the sea. Two were sold and the remaining one moved inland to stand guard alone. In 1923, the north light tower of the Chatham station was decommissioned and moved to Nauset to replace the last remaining sister. The Three Sister Lights have since been restored and are once again together in their original configuration 150 feet apart, albeit far from the sea, in a woodsy clearing off Cable Road in Eastham. The National Park Service manages these historic lights for the benefit of visitors.

Nauset Light just before moving to its current location. *Photo courtesy Shirley C. Sabin.*

Time and relentless cliff erosion threatened Nauset Light Station perched high above the ocean. After the Coast Guard proposed decommissioning the lighthouse in 1993, scores of letters poured into the Boston Coast Guard headquarters. Those who wrote pleaded for the lighthouse to be moved inland and saved. The Nauset Light Preservation Society was formed, spearheaded by several local residents. Federal grants and funds raised by the Preservation Society helped move the 90-ton tower to its new location some 336 feet inland from the old site.

Nauset Light, 2007, oil on canvas 12 x 16.

Life Saving Service

*The life saver's work is always arduous, often terrible. Quick
sands, the blinding snow and cutting sand storms, the fearful
blasts of winter gales, are more often than not to be encountered
on their journeys; storm tides, flooding the beaches, drive them to
the tops or back of the sand dunes, where they plod along their
solitary patrol with great peril.*
—J. W. Dalton, *Life Savers of Cape Cod*

Keeper Seth Ellis and his crew at the Monomoy Life Saving Station on Monomoy Island,
south of Chatham, Massachusetts. *Courtesy William P. Quinn and the U.S. Coast Guard Heritage
Museum, Barnstable, MA.*

Lighthouses considerably reduced the number of shipwrecks, but heavy fog
and blinding nor'easters with hurricane force winds still caused wrecks on Cape
shoals and sandbars. A major advance in rescuing mariners in those unfortunate
circumstances came in 1871 when the U. S. Congress created the United States
Life Saving Service. Within a year, nine stations were built on the Great Outer
Beach. At the end of the century there were a total of 13 stretching from Long
Point to Monomoy Point. These stations were manned by a keeper with a highly
trained full-time crew who could launch rescue boats from the beach into the
surf. If it was too rough to launch their boat, they would propel a line from a small
cannon onto the stricken ship and retrieve the sailors one by one by means of a
"breeches buoy." This circular flotation device with leg harness attached saved
many lives by bringing the otherwise doomed sailors ashore.

Those chosen to work as life savers were skilled and fearless seamen. Highly
regarded throughout the world for their bravery and success in rescuing lives,
they knew how to pass through the raging surf in the worst possible conditions
to rescue survivors of wrecks. On clear days watch was kept from the lookout
on the top of the station or observation points with a clear view of the beach.
Each night, or on foggy days, the men patrolled the shore by foot in search of
stranded vessels. The patrol beat was about two and a half miles distant from
each station, at which point the surfmen would meet those from the next station at a "half-way house." Here the men would get warm and exchange beach
checks. If surfmen from the neighboring station did not arrive, those patrolling
continued on to the next station or to assist the detained in a rescue.

Surf Boat Drill. Horse and crew pulling boat out of the water. 1908.
Courtesy National Park Service, Cape Cod National Sea Shore.

The life boat drill was held by the men of the U.S. Life Saving Service once or twice a week depending on sea conditions. *Courtesy William P. Quinn and the U.S. Coast Guard Heritage Museum, Barnstable, MA.*

The Old Harbor Life Saving Station was built in 1897, and is now located in Provincetown. It originally stood at the entrance of Chatham Old Harbor on Nauset Beach, but was moved in 1977 when threatened by shoreline erosion. When the station was in service it was equipped with two surf boats, two beach carts, a breeches-buoy and a life car. During the winter, a horse was kept in a nearby barn to assist the men.

Old Harbor Life Saving Station, 2008, oil on panel, 8 x 10.

United States Coast Guard

*I commend the Coast Guard on its many accomplishments, including over
one million lives saved – and counting daily – since Aug. 4, 1790.*
—Homeland Security Secretary Michael Chertoff on the 218th birthday of the U.S. Coast Guard

The U.S. Coast Guard traces its beginnings back to 1790 when Congress authorized the establishment of ten maritime vessels to enforce trade laws, prevent smuggling and collect tariffs. Known as the Revenue Cutter Service, it merged with the U.S. Life Saving Service in 1915 to become the U.S. Coast Guard. The Guard's oldest operation is search and rescue, with stations, boats, and aircraft in a constant state of readiness to meet emergency needs. The Guard is also responsible for maintaining marine aids to navigation including lighthouses, range lights, fog signals and floating buoys. Other duties include protecting against illegal fishing and destruction of maritime resources.

Facing due east above the North Atlantic Ocean and the Great Outer Beach, the former U.S. Coast Guard Station in Eastham is a majestic sight. The stately structure presents a strong and able presence in the face of the harsh surrounding environment. The wide expanse of sea it overlooks is the legendary graveyard of thousands of ancient ship wrecks. The building was erected in 1937 and remained in service as a Coast Guard station until 1958. The first headquarters of the Cape Cod National Seashore opened in this historic building in 1961. Since the National Park Service moved its seashore headquarters to Salt Pond, the former Coast Guard station currently houses the NEED (National Environmental Educational Development) Program of the Cape Cod National Seashore. Offering accommodations for up to 35 people, participants enjoy a unique opportunity to study nature and history first hand. They learn about the environment and important considerations to keep it healthy.

In 2003 the U.S. Coast Guard, described by Transportation Secretary Norman Mineta, as "one of our nation's finest treasures" was placed under the jurisdiction of the newly created Department of Homeland Security.

Former Coast Guard Station, Eastham, MA, 2007, oil on panel, 12 x 16.

Train Station in Provincetown, before 1912. *Courtesy Nickerson Archives, Cape Cod Community College.*

CHAPTER EIGHT
REALIZING DREAMS

I have been impressed with the urgency of doing. Knowing is not enough; we must apply. Being willing is not enough; we must do.
——Leonardo da Vinci

Introduction

Train Station in Orleans, c.1880. *Courtesy Nickerson Archives, Cape Cod Community College.*

Throughout Cape Cod's history there have been individuals inspired to make life easier, better, or promote the common good. Already mentioned was Henry Sears and his development of salt manufacturing by solar evaporation. In the beginning it was ridiculed as "Sears' Folly." Yet, he persisted in spite of derision and created an industry that was vital to the growth and economy of the Cape. Other individuals may have been inspired, but lacked the wherewithal to carry their dreams to fruition. Following are developments that were successful and merit attention either because they benefited Cape Cod or brought it world wide acclaim.

The Railroad

Most agree the railroad was a key factor in the growth of America. So it was with the development of Cape Cod and the neighboring islands. For those living in this area, the rails connected them to the rest of the country. Trains permitted the fisherman, cranberry grower, and Sandwich glassmaker to send their goods to greater markets more easily. Large numbers of middle class Americans could now travel to the Cape and Islands for summer seaside vacations. The first time a train arrived at a Cape Cod station was late May of 1848 when it pulled into Sandwich. Robert H. Farson in *Cape Cod Railroads* notes, "The railroad wasn't interested in [just] keeping the end of track in Sandwich, there was too much waiting farther east…" Subsequently the railroad was extended through the town of Barnstable to Main Street in Hyannis. The first passenger train arrived in Hyannis on a warm Saturday evening on July 8, 1854, and was greeted by a cheering crowd of 3,000. By September of that year a one-thousand foot wharf was completed in Hyannis where steamers could land to unload passengers and cargo. Connecting steamboat service to Nantucket began late that September.

An elegant rail station was built in Hyannis. Upstairs were offices that served as headquarters, and downstairs was a luxurious "Ladies Saloon." Nothing to do with alcohol, it was more of a tasteful parlor, furnished by the women of Hyannis. Stylish chairs, sofas, and tables afforded a pleasant surrounding for them and their children as they waited for trains. Tracks were eventually extended through the length of the Cape and reached Provincetown in 1873. The railroad operated until the mid-1960s when service was discontinued east of Yarmouth. The Commonwealth bought that right-of-way for one dollar and converted the tracks into trails for pedestrian and bike use. Currently the Cape Cod Rail Trail provides 22 miles of well paved walking and biking paths extending from Dennis to Wellfleet. The Cape Cod Central Railroad still operates scenic excursions and dinner trains from Hyannis to Buzzards Bay.

Cataumet Train Station, 2005, oil on canvas, 8 x 10.

Marconi's Wireless

In 1884, as a youth of ten, Guglielmo Marconi was fascinated by electricity. At age 16, experimenting in his parent's garden in Italy, he developed a method of sending and receiving Morse code messages. Experts at the time said it was impossible to send signals over a hill and much less over the horizon because of the curvature of the earth. Without technical knowledge but a willingness to experiment, Marconi found wireless communication could be achieved. At first, it was for short distances, but then extended longer, even over the horizon. His scientific curiosity, along with experimenting and improving technologies developed by others, led to his success building a wireless station in Wellfleet. His goal was to communicate across the vast reaches of the sea. Marconi's quest became reality when the first message, was transmitted 3,000 miles across the Atlantic Ocean. It read:

> *His Majesty, Edward VII. London, Eng.*
> *In taking advantage of the wonderful triumph of scientific research and ingenuity which has been achieved in perfecting a system of wireless telegraphy, I extend on behalf of the American people most cordial greetings and good wishes to you and to all the people of the British Empire.*
> Theodore Roosevelt, Wellfleet, Mass. Jan. 19, 1903.

Marconi succeeded when others said it would never work. Even though the original intent of the wireless station was to serve as a link between the United States and England, it would prove to be even more important for "ship to shore" communication. The Cape Cod station conveyed not only news and personal messages, but was invaluable for weather forecasts and summoning emergency aide to ships in distress. Marconi's wireless played a significant role in preventing further loss of life of passengers on the ill-fated Titanic. Although the Wellfleet station was off the air when the ship sent out its first "SOS," other operators on the rescue ship *Carpathia* were able to maintain contact through wireless communication. Marconi's equipment then helped save 712 lives.

As early as 1916, cliff erosion threatened the antenna tower bases, even though they were originally set back 165-feet from the edge when built. The station was dismantled and by 1920 was "nothing but an abandoned hulk." Today's cell phones, satellite TV and iPODS owe their origins to Marconi's development of wireless communication. In 1961 the National Park Service acquired the site as part of the Cape Cod National Seashore. Marconi Beach is open year-round with an exhibit that houses a scale model of the wireless station.

Marconi's Wireless Telegraph Experimental Station, South Wellfleet, MA.
Courtesy National Park Service, Cape Cod National Sea Shore.

Cape Wind

In the early 19th century windmills were spread over the entire Cape landscape. They ground corn and were used extensively to pump sea water for hundreds of salt works vital to the Cape economy. Jim Gordon, an experienced power plant developer, and 21st century visionary would like to see the return of wind power. By harnessing the forceful winds of Nantucket Sound on the southern border of Cape Cod, he realizes the potential of generating clean, renewable electricity. His company, Cape Wind Associates, announced a plan to build America's first offshore wind farm in 2001. The project can provide 75% of the electrical needs of the Cape and Islands. One hundred and thirty slender turbines generating on average 170 megawatts and a peak output of 420 megawatts of renewable power would be spread a half mile apart over 24 square miles. Gordon relates, "While this project is only a first step, it's a significant one toward lowering United States' dependence on foreign oil. Also important, it would reduce harmful air pollution that otherwise would come from oil and coal burning power plants." The wind farm will avoid carbon dioxide emissions by almost a million tons per year by replacing fossil fuels.

Unlike the 1800s when there were no permitting requirements to put up a windmill, Cape Wind has undergone seven years of investigation by at least fifteen local, state and federal permitting agencies. Dozens of environmental groups including the Conservation Law Foundation, Greenpeace and the Union of Concerned Scientists support the project. Although polls indicate most people are in favor of wind power and clean energy, a powerful group of citizens on Cape Cod and the Islands are concerned about visual appearance and property values. They have formed a group to oppose the project. Thousands of others have organized to support the project's merits. It's a very divisive issue locally and as the drama plays out only time will reveal the outcome of Jim Gordon's dream.

Simulation of the proposed Nantucket wind farm as seen from Cotuit, MA. *Courtesy Jim Gordon.*

The Cape Cod Canal

Miles Standish, Commander of the Plymouth settlement was first to have the idea of building a canal through the narrow neck of land between the Manomet River on Buzzards Bay and the Scusset River on Cape Cod Bay. Trade for needed supplies would be enhanced if there were a quicker and safer way to avoid the dangerous shoals in the waters surrounding the outer reaches of the Cape. Years later in 1776, when the British Navy commanded those outside waters, George Washington explored the possibility of building a canal "to give greater security to navigation against the enemy."

In the 1800s as America's industrial growth mushroomed, manufactured goods from New England needed to reach the southern colonies. Coal and lumber from southern states were essential for northern factories and homes. In his book, *The Cape Cod Canal*, Robert H. Farson wrote:

By the 1890s more than thirty thousand ships per year rounded Cape Cod; there were steamers, schooners and square riggers, United States Navy vessels, fishing boats, yachts, and strings of coastal barges. Most of them sailed through Nantucket Sound, a mariner's nightmare of shoals, twisting channels, surging tides and currents, ice and a long lee shore without ports of refuge.

Fog was particularly dreaded. A ship might anchor, but with weak kerosene lamps and hand-held fog horns, the risk of collision by a passing large steamer was great. It wasn't until 1907, that New York financier Augustus Belmont formed the Cape Cod Construction Company and successful digging began. It took seven years of dangerous and difficult work to remove the earth. Dredging got rid of the softer surface material, but had to be followed by the slow, expensive and noisy process of dynamiting massive ice-age boulders. Workers were always racing against bad weather and the need to curtail work in the winter. Finally completed, the Cape Cod Canal officially opened on July 29, 1914, a mere seventeen days before the Panama Canal. It would save seventy miles off the distance between Boston and New York. Belmont in his 80-foot yacht led a grand parade of ships, boats, and a U.S. Navy destroyer with Assistant Secretary of the Navy Franklin Delano Roosevelt on board.

Unfortunately, the canal did not live up to Belmont's expectations. It was expensive for mariners; a schooner's toll was $16, costly at the time. The shallow depth of the canal excluded passage by larger vessels which continued to sail around the cape. It became a losing proposition for Belmont and he sold the Canal to the U.S. government in 1928 for $11.5 million. Soon after, the 17.4 mile canal was widened to nearly 500 feet and deepened to 32 feet. Today the Army Corps of Engineers operates and maintains the canal and over 20,000 vessels of all types use the waterway annually.

Cape Cod Canal, 2008, oil on panel, 9 x 12.

Marine Biological Laboratory

The seaside village of Woods Hole in Falmouth is an unusual mix of weathered fishermen and world renowned scientists. The Marine Biological Laboratory, or MBL, as the organization is known locally, was conceived in 1886 by Spencer Fullerton Baird, the country's first Fish Commissioner. He had a research station in Woods Hole and wanted to expand it into a major research laboratory. He encouraged Alpheus Hyatt, who had a marine biology laboratory in Annisquam, Massachusetts, to join him. To help finance the project, the Women's Education Association of Boston invited the country's leading biologists to a meeting at the Boston Society of Natural History. The meeting was attended by professors from Harvard, MIT and Williams College. A committee was formed and it shaped plans for the organization of a permanent seaside laboratory.

Lectures and an operetta were held to raise funds. This along with money from 83 subscribers and donors from the Women's Education As-

sociation raised $10,000. Woods Hole was selected as the site and a small parcel of land was purchased. A modest 28 by 63 foot shingled building was erected and the MBL was incorporated in March 1888. Charles Otis Whitman, an embryologist, was the first director of the MBL. He emphasized the need to combine research and education at the new facility. Work began with a mere seven investigators and eight students attending the first session. The first summer offering was a six-week introductory course on invertebrate zoology. From the very start trustees envisioned visiting researchers coming from all parts of the country. Indeed, today, hundreds of world class scientists and researchers come to the MBL to work and study. Over fifty Nobel Laureates have been associated with the MBL and have furthered the organization's mission to "improve the human condition through basic research and education in biology, biomedicine, and environmental science."

The Candle House, Woods Hole, MA. A former 19th century stone spermaceti candle factory houses the administrative offices of the Marine Biological Laboratory, Woods Hole, MA.

Woods Hole Oceanographic Institution

Another world class facility, the Woods Hole Oceanographic Institute is dedicated to ocean research, education, and exploration. It was founded in 1930 as a result of a committee of the National Academy of Science concluding it was time "to consider the share of the United States of America in a worldwide program of oceanographic research." The Rockefeller Foundation bestowed a $3 million grant to support the work of scientists, construction of a laboratory and commissioning of a research vessel. In that first year, trustees authorized $175,000 for construction of a 142-foot steel hulled ketch. The *Atlantis*, as it was named, was equipped with two laboratories, accommodations for six scientists and dormitory space for students as well as crew. A four story brick laboratory was also built and later named for the founding director of the institution, Henry Bigelow.

During World War II, WHOI scientists played a significant role in maritime and national defense. Many U.S. Navy operations depended on knowledge of the ocean environment. Navy sponsored WHOI programs included studying the effects of water temperature and salinity on transmission of underwater sound, prevention of marine fouling on hulls of vessels, and study of underwater explosives. The 60 summertime staff almost doubled to 100 and the budget soared to over one million dollars. The National Science Foundation first called on WHOI workers in 1952 to study summer plankton growth in Long Island bays. Over the years NSF funding for research has surpassed that of the U.S. Office of Naval Research. Today, WHOI's staff and student body number close to a thousand. Through a joint program with the Massachusetts Institute of Technology, the institution has granted over 600 doctoral, masters and engineering degrees in oceanography. WHOI currently operates three large research vessels, *Atlantis*, *Knorr*, and *Oceanus*, several smaller boats, the three-person submersible *Alvin*, and a fleet of remotely-operated underwater vehicles. From an inauspicious summer laboratory, WHOI has become the world's largest private, nonprofit ocean research and education organization. Venturing into oceans all over the world, research includes geological activity, global climate change, ocean pollution and study of plant animal and microbial organisms.

R/V Tioga, Woods Hole Oceanographic Institution, Woods Hole, MA.
WHOI's aluminum hulled coastal research vessel serves ocean scientists and engineers working in the waters of the Northeastern United States.

Where I Want to Be (view from the Wequassett Inn, Chatham, MA), 2006, oil on panel, 9 x12.

CHAPTER NINE
THE LURE OF CAPE COD

The world of strife seems far away. It must have been a kindly God
who shaped the sands of old Cape Cod.
—Ferdinand C. Land, On Old Cape Cod

Introduction

Until the 19th century, visitors to Cape Cod were few. Those who came found travel by stagecoach difficult and exhausting. Although there were a few sportsmen who came to hunt or the likes of Henry David Thoreau, who explored this little known area, tourism was insignificant. The Methodist summer camp meetings set the stage for attracting large numbers of people. Beginning at the tip of the Cape in Wellfleet in 1819, the outdoor tent meetings attracted those drawn to the informal discourses of zealous preachers. Later, when the revival meetings moved to Eastham's Millennium Grove in 1828, as many as five thousand people came and listened for hours to the scores of preachers who spoke. Most attendees were women who welcomed trading the drudgery of housework for inspiration. Within a few years, when the meetings moved further up Cape close to the new railroad station in Yarmouth, large numbers of attendees came from off-Cape.

During and after the Civil War, the Cape economy declined drastically. Fishing and maritime activities waned, manufacturing slumped, and saltworks that had covered the land were gone. Entrepreneurs, recognizing the attraction of the sea and shore, as well as the Cape's rustic charm, began to purchase cheap land and erect hotels and summer cottages. Most of the early Cape Cod summer hotels were on the south side, particularly in the Falmouth area because of its extensive shoreline. The period of large inns thrived for a half-century beginning in the 1870s. The early hotels were made of wood, simply furnished, and provided only minimal amenities permitting owners to turn a profit during the short 12-week summer period.

Quisset Harbor House, between Falmouth and Woods Hole, was considered one of the most prestigious places to stay, yet for many decades did not even have running water. The stoneware basin with hot water sent up in the mornings was part of the charm. Other areas of the Cape boasted fine lodgings: the Cotuit Inn, Chatham Bars Inn, Wellfleet's Chequesset Inn and Provincetown's Red Inn are just a few historic vacation destinations. Visitors to these resort hotels did not have to venture beyond the boundaries. Meals were included and tended to be elaborate affairs. As hotels developed, they added tennis courts, billiard rooms, and golf links to the standard croquet set. Clambakes, fishing, and catboat sailing became the rage. It wasn't until automobile use became popular that summer visitors could venture beyond the hotel confines and enjoy all the region had to offer. Along with the development of hotels, summer cottages became a booming business. Today, visitors to the Cape not only enjoy extraordinary natural beauty, but a wide range of activities for every taste.

National Seashore

Forces of nature have taken considerable oceanfront terrain and will continue to do so, but the creation of the Cape Cod National Seashore ensures that much of the remaining coastal land will not be developed and historic resources will be preserved. Signed into law by President John F. Kennedy on August 7, 1961, the park's forty-mile stretch of protected territory includes land from the southern tip of Nauset Beach in Chatham to Long Point in Provincetown. Public use of the land allows visitors to enjoy an endless choice of activities. The park includes swimming beaches, tidal flats, high cliff dunes, and salt marshes. Inland there are walking and biking woodland trails, kettle ponds, and wild cranberry bogs. The varied terrain supports diverse species of birds and animals. The National Park Service manages the National Seashore. Open daily, year round from 9 a.m. to 4:30 p.m., the Salt Pond Visitors Center in Eastham and its friendly rangers provide helpful information as well as in-depth programs.

Cape Cod National Seashore. *Map adapted from National Park Service Handbook by Liz Kleekamp.*

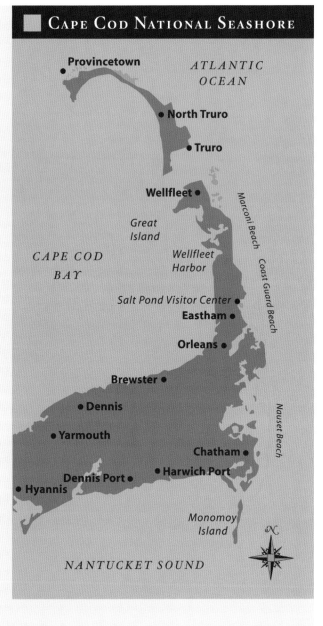

CAPE COD NATIONAL SEASHORE

Provincetown

ATLANTIC OCEAN

North Truro

Truro

Wellfleet

Marconi Beach

Great Island

Wellfleet Harbor

Coast Guard Beach

CAPE COD BAY

Salt Pond Visitor Center

Eastham

Orleans

Brewster

Nauset Beach

Dennis

Yarmouth

Chatham

Dennis Port

Harwich Port

Hyannis

Monomoy Island

NANTUCKET SOUND

Celebrations

Fourth of July festivities in every Cape town kick off the summer season. Activities fill the day from sunrise to well into the night. In the town of Sandwich, an early morning road race starts the day. By 9:30, hundreds of children on gaily decorated bikes and wagons are ready to parade down Main Street. Marching bands, floats, antique cars, local politicians and blaring fire trucks follow. After the parade, kids of all ages work off steam in competitive water games on a nearby athletic field. The evening ends with a magical boat parade on historic Shawme Pond. This colorful event, with oriental lantern-festooned rowboats and other small craft, had its beginning over a century ago.

July 4th in Sandwich, 2004, oil on canvas, 12 x 24.

Architecture

One of the most striking aspects of the Cape is its architectural heritage. Timothy Dwight, president of Yale University coined the name "Cape Cod house" when he toured the area in 1800. Unadorned and practical as the early settlers who first built it, the house provided shelter, but also had to hold up to harsh sea winds and fierce nor'easters. Built close to the ground, with a steep pitched roof, its multi-paned windows were placed directly under the eaves. The large central chimney not only provided warmth, but was the mainstay of the house. A fine example of the "full-cape" house is the Atwood Higgins House nestled in a tiny hamlet of barns and outbuildings just off Pamet Road in Wellfleet. Like many Cape cottages, the Atwood Higgins House started out as a humble half-house built by Thomas Atwood in 1730. Often, the small cottages grew, from a one or two-room structure, or "half-Cape" to a seven or eight room "full-Cape" as did Atwood's. In between, as young families grew, a room might be added to the original small dwelling resulting in the "three quarter-Cape." The historic Atwood-Higgins house is managed by the National Park Service and seasonal tours are offered to visitors.

The Atwood Higgins House, Wellfleet, MA, 2006, oil on canvas, 11 x 14.

The Hoxie House, Sandwich, MA, 2003, oil on canvas, 9 x 12.

The "salt-box" house is another style of dwelling that appeared early Cape Cod. A fine example is the beautifully restored Hoxie House in the town of Sandwich. Dating back to the mid-1600s, it sits on a bluff overlooking ancient Shawme Pond. Named after the old-fashioned salt container it resembles, it is characterized by a short front roof and deep sloped back. The design was practical, permitting the back roof to take the brunt of winter storms, allow-ing snow to slide off easily. In spite of its somewhat foreboding exterior, the moment one enters the keeping room of the Hoxie House, with its massive brick fireplace and wide plank floors, one can easily envision the warmth and coziness enjoyed by its 17th century occupants. The Hoxie House is open to the public from May to October with guides offering tours.

A Special Place

Every visitor to the Cape has a particular place that evokes a special memory. For those who vacation or live on the Upper-Cape, the Sandwich Boardwalk is such a place. Stretching over unspoiled marshland, meandering saltwater inlets and sandy tidal shores, this unique 1,350-foot long structure ends on the dunes with a panoramic view of the sea. It was first built in 1875 by Gustavus Howland, a lumber dealer and builder. He felt a walkway would be an enjoyable way for early tourists to reach and enjoy the stunning views of Cape Cod Bay. Battered over the years by fierce winds and storms, the original boardwalk has been rebuilt several times. After Hurricane Bob wiped it out in 1991, townspeople thought of a creative way to raise funds. Over 1,700 individual planks were bought and engraved with the purchaser's message of choice. Completely funded by these private donations the new boardwalk was completed in 1992 and once again replanked in 2003.

Boardwalk Sunrise, 2007, oil on canvas, 9 x 12.

High Tide at the Boardwalk, 2003, oil on canvas, 11 x 14.

Jumping into the water from the Sandwich Boardwalk is a rite of passage for every youth in town. For those who prefer walking to jumping, the engravings on the planks offer an entertaining glimpse into the stories of townspeople. There's the summons to "Fly high and free, sis," an admonition to "The fat Grandpa," a tender "I love you Paul." One of the most inviting planks is "Meet here," the invitation to visit often. To reach the Boardwalk, follow Route 6A to Jarves Street. The Boardwalk is located at the end of Jarves and Harbor Streets.

Cape Cod Trails

A cyclist's paradise, Cape Cod offers hundreds of miles of dedicated bike trails along waterways, marshes, and inland forests. The Cape Cod Canal bikeways run along both sides of the canal and offer a unique vantage point to view the Sagamore and Bourne Bridges. The paved Cape Cod Rail Trail follows a former railroad track for 22 miles from Dennis to Wellfleet. Pristine lakes, woodlands, and cranberry bogs enhance the outlook and a wide shoulder also accommodates walkers, runners and horseback riders. The Shining Sea Trail from Jones Road in Falmouth to Woods Hole runs directly along Vineyard Sound in some areas allowing bikers to stop for a picnic on the beach. The 10 miles of Nickerson State Park Trails are convenient to woodland picnicking and swimming. Some of the most beautiful scenery is evident on the National Seashore Trail with its paths winding through uplands, over marshland, and close to the sea and dunes.

The Cyclists, 2006, watercolor on paper, 14 x 18.

Sailing

For centuries, people have enjoyed recreational sailing on Cape Cod Bay and Nantucket Sound. For some, it's the thrill of pitting oneself against the forces of nature; for others the challenge of rounding the next marker before an opponent. For many, it's just the sheer pleasure of being surrounded by water with friends or family enjoying a breezy summer day.

Sport Fishing

The sport fishing season on Cape Cod begins in early spring, sometimes as soon as April for early striped bass in the surrounding waters. Bluefish are soon to follow and it's not unusual for anglers to be spotted at all hours of the day on beaches and canal side for their shot at a trophy catch. For those who prefer deep sea fishing, just about every town has charter boats, often piloted by retired professional fishermen and enthusiasts of the sport. Fighting a giant tuna with rod and reel is the ultimate test of skill and endurance.

Coming Home, 2007, oil on canvas, 9 x 12.

Best of Times, 2006, oil on canvas, 8 x 10.

For those seeking solitude or a peaceful spot away from the din of everyday life, one doesn't have to go far on Cape Cod. A weathered bench can be just as inviting as fresh painted Adirondack chairs to view mesmerizing vistas of land and sea.

A Calming Place, 2005, oil on canvas, 8 x 10.

Chatham Bars with Hydrangeas, 2005, oil on canvas, 12 x 16.

Favorite Tee, 2006,
oil on panel, 8 x 10.

Golf

Some say golf is essentially a seaside game and that a wind-swept coastal link adds challenge to the sport. Cape Cod and the Islands offer premier golf destinations with over fifty courses, including over two dozen public venues to choose from. Each has a distinctive history and character. Highland Links, founded in 1892 is the oldest on Cape Cod. Sitting high on the bluffs with a spectacular view of the Atlantic Ocean, it is a "genuine" link close to the Scottish tradition. The Cummaquid Golf Club was "carved from a cow pasture" in 1895 by a group of enthusiasts of the sport. No matter which course is selected, the player is guaranteed a stimulating challenge in a beautiful setting.

Art and Artists

Charles W. Hawthorne's Cape Cod School of Art, which opened in 1898, led the way to Provincetown becoming the "biggest art colony in the world." Hawthorne and his students, who painted outdoors, were attracted by the exceptional quality of the natural light and the charm of the historic fishing village. By 1916 there were five summer art schools and during the 1930s and 1940s, world-class abstract expressionists such as Robert Motherwell, Hans Hofmann, and Willem de Kooning spent summers there. The visual splendor and inspirational forces of Cape Cod still attract artists, writers and poets. Over 300 galleries spread over the Cape afford collectors an opportunity to purchase original artwork. Institutions like the Cape Cod Museum of Art, Provincetown Art Association and Museum, Cape Cod Art Association and the Falmouth Artists' Guild provide ongoing exhibitions and classes for all skill levels. Several towns, including Sandwich, Chatham and Falmouth, have local artist associations that hold outdoor shows in the summer months.

Charles W. Hawthorne and Students. Provincetown, 1915. *Courtesy Provincetown Art Association and Museum.*

Under the Tent, 2007, oil on canvas, 11 x 14.

Performing Arts

In the early part of the 20th century the isolation of Provincetown and vacant fishing shanties were a great attraction to writers and playwrights. In 1916 the concept for the historic Provincetown Players was developed by George Cook and his wife, Susan Glaspell. They were interested in starting a new type of theater in America that would deal with contemporary issues more realistically than they were then being portrayed. What started out as a group of friends performing at home for their own amusement led to presenting plays in the makeshift Wharf Theater, a converted fish house. Interest escalated and many others from the New York theater community made summer pilgrimages to the Cape. Eugene O'Neill's first play, *Bound East for Cardiff,* had its debut at the Wharf Theater. Decades later other debuts were made including a young Marlon Brando playing the part of Stanley Kowalski in Tennessee Williams's new play, *A Streetcar Named Desire*. Richard Gere made his debut at the Theater on the Wharf in Tom Stoppard's *Rosenkrantz and Guildenstern Are Dead.*

In 1927, after spending several summers working in the Provincetown theater scene, Raymond Moore decided to open his own professional summer theater. He bought a former Unitarian meeting house, moved it to spacious pasture land off historic Old Kings Highway in Dennis and converted it to a playhouse. Over the years performers at the Cape Playhouse have included almost every well known actor of stage and screen including a teenaged Jane Fonda, a young Jimmy Stewart, and usherette Bette Davis. The theater is still a vibrant organization presenting more than a half-dozen plays each summer.

Provincetown Fishermen's Quarters, before 1912. Buildings like these were later converted to artist galleries or theaters. *Courtesy Nickerson Archives, Cape Cod Community College.*

Literary Arts

For the past 46 years, during the third week in August, writers of all levels of experience gather at the Cape Cod Writers' Center. Located in the tiny Victorian hamlet of Craigville in the village of Centerville, this nationally recognized conference offers courses in fiction, creative non-fiction, poetry, editing, and publishing. Guest lecturers, master classes, poetry and prose readings inspire attendees. Speakers have included Kurt Vonnegut Jr., Mary Higgins Clark, Robert Finch, Art Buchwald, and many other acclaimed authors.

Shopping

From Falmouth Village on the Upper-Cape to Provincetown at land's end, charming shops and galleries line the main street in every village. Tourism drives the Cape economy and businesses cater to every conceivable visitor need. Chatham, with its flower-decked storefronts, provides enjoyment even for window shoppers. When energy is exhausted, there are ample restaurants, ice cream, and candy shops for refueling. There is also the Cape Cod Mall in Hyannis, especially popular on rainy days.

Main Street, Chatham, MA, 2005, oil on canvas, 9 x 12.

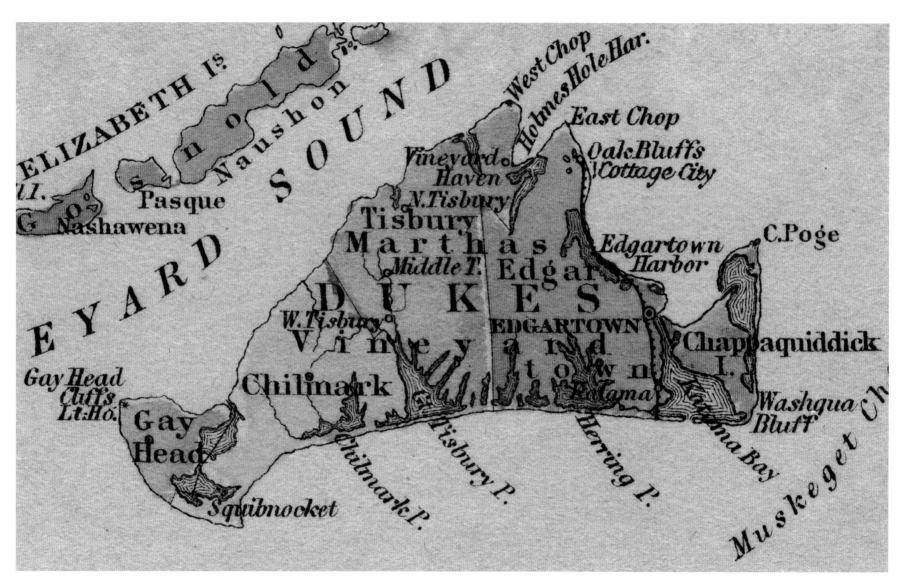

Martha's Vineyard. Frank A. Gray, map author, 1881.

CHAPTER TEN
MARTHA'S VINEYARD

In Vineyard Haven, on Martha's Vineyard, mostly I love the soft collision here of harbor and shore, the subtly haunting briny quality that all small towns have when they are situated on the sea.
—William Styron

Introduction

Martha's Vineyard, located seven miles off the south coast of Cape Cod, is an island of extraordinary beauty. Twenty-four miles long and ten miles wide, the island features cliffs, sandy beaches, meadows and coastal plains, all embraced by surrounding ocean. Much of the island's interior natural pasture lands and wooded hills are preserved as conservation area. Each of the six towns that make up the Vineyard has its own distinct character, unique history and charm.

Edgartown, today an exquisitely maintained seaport village, was the first colonial settlement on the island. First known as Great Harbour, it came into its own at the height of the whaling industry. The stately sea captain homes that line north Water Street reflect the heritage and success of its shipmasters. Other dwellings like the 1672 Vincent House, now a museum, reflect a simpler way of life that most on the island experienced. Oak Bluffs, named for its picturesque setting, is a community that formed around Methodist revival camp meetings. Those who first came to find God stayed for nature's splendor.

As unique carpenter-Gothic cottages replaced early tents and entrepreneurs developed the land, the face of Martha's Vineyard would change forever.

Vineyard Haven (also known as Tisbury) was once one of New England's busiest ports. Originally called "Holmes Hole," it is the primary point of entry to the island. The entrance to Vineyard Haven is marked by two spits of land, West Chop, on the northern tip of the town, and East Chop, across the harbor on the northern tip of Oak Bluffs. These three most populous areas are known by the locals as "down-island." The more western rural towns of West Tisbury, Chilmark (including the fishing village of Menemsha), and Aquinnah are familiarly known as "up-island." The terms "up-island" and "down-island" are derived from nautical terminology: the further west one travels, the higher the longitude. Chappaquiddick Island is a part of Edgartown separated by a mere 300-yard wide strait. The name comes from the Indian "cheppiaquidne" meaning "separated island." Martha's Vineyard, Chappaquiddick and the Elizabeth Islands together make up Dukes County.

Timothy Coffin House, 1828, Edgartown.

Vineyard Haven Harbor.

Menemsha Harbor.

Early Settlement

The native Wampanoags called the island *Noepe* or "land amid the streams," a fitting name for this largest island in New England. Wise stewards, the Wampanoags knew how to farm the land and when to let it lie fallow in order to harvest a rich bounty. As a result, when Bartholomew Gosnold explored the island in 1602, his chronicler described it as a "place most pleasant" appreciating the abundant woods, wild grape vines, and berry bushes. Legend tells us Gosnold named the island Martha's Vineyard in honor of either his mother-in-law or infant daughter who were both named Martha. However, at least one historian disputes that story. Charles Edward Banks, M.D., author of *The History of Martha's Vineyard*, says the name that was used up to the year 1700 was "Martin's Island." He cites writings of local historians as well as its early governor, and speculates it may have been named after Gosnold's shipmate, Captain John Martin. At some point in the early 1700s, the name Martha's Vineyard took hold.

In 1641, Thomas Mayhew, an English merchant from Watertown, Massachusetts, purchased settlement rights to Martha's Vineyard, Nantucket, and the Elizabeth Islands. Shortly after, Mayhew's son, 21-year old Thomas Jr., along with several others from Watertown, settled in an area they called Great Harbor, today's Edgartown. According to historian Henry Norton, young Mayhew was resolute about the need to "purchase" any land taken from native Wampanoags. The elder Mayhew arrived in 1646 with his second wife and five children. It took seven years for a town government to be established and when it was, most leaders were members of the Mayhew family. In the absence of a minister, Thomas Jr. accepted the responsibility. He successfully converted a native named Hiacoomes, who taught him how to speak the Algonquian language. Young Mayhew then traveled all over the Vineyard preaching to the natives. In 1651 he established the first school on the Vineyard to teach children and "any of the young Indian men who were willing to learn." Peter Folger, who later became the grandfather of Benjamin Franklin, was the first teacher. He found the natives "quick to learn and willing to be instructed in the ways of the English."

In 1657, young Mayhew, after spending a week with his Indian converts embarked on a short trip to England to share his experiences working with the natives. With him were his wife's brother and Caleb Chesschamuck, the first Indian graduate of Harvard University. Norton writes, "The Indians stood on the beach with bowed heads" watching the ship depart. Sadly, Mayhew's ship and passengers were lost at sea and never heard from again. His legacy however, led to missionary work that would extend through five generations of Mayhews.

For the most part, the early colonists were of English stock and lived as did their counterparts in England but were constrained by local circumstances and resources. Homes were one-story, with frames of pine or oak which grew nearby. Low to the ground with very large fireplaces, they were always located near springs of fresh water. Most of the settlers kept sheep and oxen and the tallow from these animals was made into candles. As whaling developed and Vineyard captains brought home their harvest of whale oil, spermaceti candles came into use. Edgartown at one time had the largest spermaceti candle factory in America.

The 1672 Vincent House, built in Edgartown, is the oldest house on Martha's Vineyard.

Since there was no real currency in those early days, bartering was common. Norton relates that Islanders would exchange home-made mittens, cookies, pies, and other things for "molasses, sugar, ginger, spices and Holland rum."

Marriage was performed purely as a civil ceremony, expressing the colonists desire to be free of religious customs. It was not until well into the 18th century that marriage was solemnized by clergymen. Class distinctions were present. In his official role, Thomas Mayhew was referred to as "worshipful." Persons of gentle birth were addressed as Master or Mister, and the next lower designation was as "Goodman." The lowest class was simply addressed by name without any prefix; e.g., John Brown. This ended when the Declaration of Independence indicated all men were "born free and equal." In 1671 the area was incorporated as Edgar Towne, after Edgar, son of the Duke of York.

One of the first things the colonists did was build schools. Even before Thomas Mayhew Jr. built his school for the natives, there had been a school to teach English children. One of the finest schools of the 18th century was in Edgartown and kept by Reverend Joseph Thaxter, pastor of the Congregational Church and first chaplain of the United States Army. Parson Thaxter's students were required to study Latin from the age of seven.

Native Wampanoags

When Europeans first dropped anchor off the shores of Martha's Vineyard in the 1500s, there were over three thousand native Wampanoags living on the island. Their tribal ancestors had inhabited the land for over 10,000 years. By the 1700s when much of the island was settled by the English, the native population was greatly reduced. As land was bought by the white settlers, their new models of private land ownership conflicted with the tribe's communal practices. Large areas of hunting grounds were lost and disease virtually wiped out entire native villages. By 1800 there were only about 330 natives left who lived primarily in Aquinnah, Christiantown (West Tisbury), and Chappaquiddick. Today that number remains approximately the same for those living on the island. Others have since moved off island. In spite of their diminished numbers, Wampanoag influence is strongly felt on the Vineyard. Helped by 1987 federal legislation, the Gay Head Wampanoags were granted return of tribal lands and eligibility for grants to build housing and administration offices. Native names identify ancient roads, lakes and districts.

Wampanoags are governed by a Tribal Council which includes a Chief, Medicine Man, and council members. All hold these positions for life. The language is taught to tribal members and many customs and commemorations continue. The annual summer "Legends of Moshup" pageant depicts the folklore and stories surrounding the ancient Wampanoag giant. In early October there is the "Cranberry Day" celebration. Wild cranberries grow on 200 acres of tribal land and each year children are excused from school and along with elders gather cranberries and enjoy picnicking on the beach. The children are taught ancient legends and join elders to give thanks to their creator for the year's harvest. Traditional arts such as basket weaving, beadwork, and pottery making continue to be taught. These products are sold in shops managed by the Wampanoags in Aquinnah.

Martha's Vineyard and the Revolution

Islanders have historically been non-combatants in times of war, understandable since their isolated location and exposure to the sea made them vulnerable to enemies. During the Revolutionary War they, like their neighbors on Cape Cod and Nantucket, were helpless in the face of the maritime supremacy of Great Britain. The vast English navy, with cannon-decked ships, was stationed only thirty-five miles away in Newport, Rhode Island. When the U.S. Congress declared independence from England in 1776, one of the issues was the Townshend Acts of 1767. That proceeding required colonists to pay a tax on glass, paint, paper, and tea. In response the colonies placed an embargo on all British goods until the Townshend Acts were repealed. Islanders hoped the embargo would work, but that was not the case and peace could not be negotiated.

Islanders worried about protecting their land as skirmishes escalated and fighting began at Lexington and Concord. Many of its young men were on ships at sea. Although many islanders initially desired neutrality, in time attitudes changed. Then most openly declared themselves for liberty. That being the case, it's easy to envision their fear, aware that British ships were sailing all along the mainland coast pillaging and destroying towns.

A major incident in that war happened when General Charles Grey and his fleet of ten thousand British troops sailed into Holmes Hole (today's Vineyard Haven) on the afternoon of September 10, 1778. Under a flag of truce, Beriah Norton, the island's top ranking military man went on board with two other islanders. British General Grey ordered 10,000 sheep and 300 oxen be delivered by 2:00 p.m. the next day. The animals were needed to feed the great numbers of British troops stationed in Rhode Island. He also called for all arms and ammunition on the island. If these demands were met, the 450 troops who meanwhile had left the transport ships and went ashore, would not bother the residents. Norton wrote in his diary that General Grey promised "payment would be made" for supplies that were to be handed over.

One can imagine the state of disorder and confusion as thousands of sheep and cattle began surging into Holmes Hole in less than a day's time. "Sullen and despairing," the residents handed over their animals, Although no shots were fired during this episode, the community suffered resulting starvation and several whale boats and a salt works were destroyed. Continuous requests for promised payment to match the number of animals taken were never fulfilled by the British.

Whaling Days

Although Martha's Vineyard did not achieve the status of Nantucket or New Bedford as an important whaling port, the industry was nonetheless a primary livelihood for Island men. It wasn't unusual for a boy of twelve or thirteen to sign on as crew member. For the most part, the ships' owners were not from Martha's Vineyard, but rather New Bedford or Nantucket. Other maritime-related industries also flourished including fishing, candle manufacturing, and salt making. Dr. Daniel Fisher was Edgartown's most successful whaling entrepreneur. He owned what is now the town wharf, a spermaceti candle factory, and a whale oil refinery. His net worth was reputed to be $250,000 and the Federal style home he built at 101 Main Street reflects his success.

Captain Daniel Fisher House built in 1840, Edgartown, MA.

Edgartown Harbor, date unknown. *Courtesy Martha's Vineyard Museum.*

Between 1835 and 1845 there were 110 whaling captains living in Edgartown. Their affluence is evident by the beautiful mansions and public buildings built during this period. The Federated Church built in 1828 is the oldest church built on the Vineyard and is still used for services. The impressive Old Whaling Church, built in 1843, is felt to be one of the finest examples of Greek Revival architecture in New England. Chappaquiddick also had a large population of whaling captains. One of these, Captain William A. Martin, born in 1829, holds the distinction of becoming the only African-American master of whaling ships on Martha's Vineyard. The great-grand child of an African woman enslaved on Martha's Vineyard, he became a highly respected shipmaster. His career spanned forty years and took him all over the world. He lived with his wife, Sarah, and her family in the area of Chappaquiddick Island known as "Indian land."

One of the most celebrated whaling families was that of Valentine Pease Jr. His father and grandfather were master mariners, as were his three brothers, one of whom perished at sea. Two of his three sisters were married to whaling captains. Captain Pease Jr. gained fame as the master of the ship *Acushnet* on which Herman Melville sailed. Many believe Valentine Pease was the prototype for Herman Melville's character Captain Ahab, in *Moby Dick*. At the height of the whaling era, forty-five master mariners, twelve of them Peases, came from the island.

Lieutenant William Cooke Pease revealed an intimate look at the hardship of leaving home and family to go to sea. He left his wife Serena and two little sons, Willie, age two, and Valentine, less than one year old. Departing Edgartown on March 29, 1850, he wrote in his diary, "To leave my wife and dear little babes, very hard. Willie stood at the door and looked melancholy as my things were being put on the coach. Poor little fellow, he little knew I was going away, although he seems to do so."

The following year would prove extremely difficult for Lieutenant Pease and his wife. Baby Valentine died and Serena fell into deep despair at the loss of her child and a husband, far away at sea. Author Florence Kern, referred to "the strained relationship of William and Serena, as they fought loneliness and grief while 3,000 miles apart."

Old Whaling Church built in 1843, Edgartown, MA.

Methodist Camp Meetings and Cottage City

Cottage City Gingerbread, c.1890.
Courtesy Martha's Vineyard Museum.

One of the most successful revivalists in early Vineyard history was John "Reformation" Adams. A dynamic and confident Methodist preacher, he lured many away from the more staid meetings at the Congregational church. One of those converted was Jeremiah Pease of Edgartown. After attending a week-long outdoor Methodist camp meeting in West Chop, Pease was inspired to establish a more permanent campground so meetings might continue. His efforts would dramatically change the course of Martha's Vineyard history.

In 1835, Pease, along with six men from the Edgartown Methodist Church chose a half-acre site that seemed a promising location for campground meetings. Situated in what was then the northern part of Edgartown, the gently sloping land was in a shady grove of oak trees. They cleared the site of underbrush and erected a shed and pulpit for the minister. A small altar was put up and beyond that there were backless wood benches. A semi-circle of society tents surrounded the outer edge.

Preaching and prayer meetings were held each day and evening. Meetings rapidly expanded as attendees usually stayed for several days, looking forward to the emotional, religious, and social rewards of their visit. On one occasion in 1853, revival meetings were held for 100 nights in succession. The original nine tents in 1835 expanded to 200 by 1855. Many of these were family tents with children, who were prohibited at first from participating, but then later allowed to attend meetings. In 1840 a lease was taken out and the area became known as Wesleyan Grove. By 1868 there were 570 tents with over 12,000 people attending meetings. In that same year the Massachusetts legislature passed an act incorporating the Martha's Vineyard Camp Meeting Association. The community of canvas homes took on the appearance of individual neighborhoods with groupings of tents.

Over the years, attendees, many from off-island, relished their island experience and desired more permanent dwellings. The campground cottage came into demand. Inexpensive, attractive, and easy to erect, there were 250 built by 1869. Called Carpenter Gothic, the houses were consistent in style, looking like miniature churches. The main entrance was usually a double door with a narrow window on both sides. The tops of these openings were either rounded or peaked. The porch ran along the entire front of the house and often a little balcony from the upstairs bedroom extended over it.

Entering the 34-acre hamlet of Cottage City in Oak Bluffs, today's first-time visitor is easily overwhelmed with wonder, curiosity, and otherworldliness. Hundreds of these diminutive two-story cottages compete for identity in a fantasy of color far beyond any imaginable artist palette. Once numbering 500, there remain 300 cottages today. In 1879 a vast open-air wrought iron tabernacle seating 1,200 people was erected, replacing the large central tent. A unique structure with wrought iron arches, dozens of colored glass windows, and an octagonal cupola, it was named to the National Register of Historic Places on its centennial anniversary in 1979. The Tabernacle is still used for cultural events. The first event of the season is the graduation ceremony of The Martha's Vineyard Regional High School.

Campground Cottages in Oak Bluffs.

Oak Bluffs Cottage, 2008, oil on panel, 12 x 16.

A Sacred Cliff

Previously known as Gay Head, Aquinnah is defined by its 150-foot cliffs. Composed of sediment from six ancient glaciers, they contain layers of red and white clay, green sand, white quartz, black soil and brownish-black lignite. In the September 1860 edition of *Harper's Magazine*, D. H. Strother wrote:

> *The rains have furrowed the face with deep gullies, leaving sharp and fantastically-shaped ridges between, and exposing various and bright colored earths—red, white, yellow, black, brown, and purple—which, in the sunshine, rejoice the eyes of the passing mariner, and have gained for it its name of Gay Head.*

A century and a half later, time and erosion have dulled the red and purple colors, but the cliffs are still a magnificent sight. The furthest point out on the cliffs is known as Devil's Den. A sacred spot in Wampanoag lore, it's where Moshup, an ancient Indian giant lived with his wife and children. The streaks of red in the cliff are believed to be from the blood of whales that Moshup dragged on land to cook. To fuel the fire, he pulled trees up by the roots leaving the cliffs without any timber – as they appear today. All of the shops and businesses on the bluff by the cliffs are owned and operated by tribal members. The Wampanoag Tribe of Gay Head (Aquinnah) became a federally acknowledged tribe on April 10, 1987. In accordance with that settlement act they were allocated approximately 480 acres of tribal lands.

Aquinnah Light, 2006, oil on canvas, 9 x 12.

Lighthouses

Martha's Vineyard is considered by some to have the most diverse group of light houses within such a limited area. All are located on the north side of the island facing Vineyard Sound, a busy thoroughfare of coastal trade in the 1700 and 1800s. The first light station to go into service was Gay Head Light (Aquinnah Light) in 1799. Ebenezer Skiff, the earliest keeper, was the first white man to live in the town of Gay Head, a Wampanoag settlement. As maritime traffic increased and the Gay Head location became increasingly important, Congress appropriated $30,000 in 1854 to build a new tower and dwelling to replace the original decaying structures. A first-order Fresnel lens containing 1,008 prisms was obtained from Paris. D.H. Strother, in *Harper's Magazine*, described the mesmerizing effect of the glass prisms lit by sperm whale oil, "Of all the heavenly phenomena that I have had the good fortune to witness—borealis lights, mock suns, or meteoric showers—I have never seen anything that, in mystic splendor, equaled this trick of the magic lantern of Gay Head."

First Order Fresnel Lens, 1854. Originally located on top of the Aquinnah Lighthouse station, it was replaced by two aerobeacons in 1952.

The Cape Poge Lighthouse, on Chappaquiddick Island was erected in 1801. Rebuilt four times and moved as many times, it has the distinction of being the first entire lighthouse to be moved to its present location by helicopter. The wooden West Chop Light in Vineyard Haven was built in 1817 and replaced by the present brick structure a little more than two decades later. The U.S. Coast Guard currently occupies the caretaker's cottage and maintains the light. The year 1828 saw the construction of two light stations: East Chop Light in Oak Bluffs and Edgartown Light. The location of the East Chop light, long known as Telegraph Hill, was the sight of a semaphore station. Using a series of flags on raised and lowered arms, the site was linked to stations in Woods Hole, Nantucket and Plymouth. Until 1988, when it was painted white, the East Chop light was known affectionately as "the chocolate lighthouse" for its brownish-red color. Edgartown light originally sat offshore on pilings. At first, the keeper had to row to the mainland for supplies. In 1830, a wooden causeway was built to the lighthouse at a cost of $2,500. The causeway became known locally as the "Bridge of Sighs," because men about to leave on whaling voyages would frequently walk there with their wives or girl friends. Over the years, the dwelling and walkway were damaged and had to be repaired many times. A hurricane in 1938 was a final blow and the building was demolished by the Lighthouse Service in 1939. A 45-foot cast iron tower on Crane's Beach in Ipswich, Massachusetts was disassembled and carried by barge to Edgartown Harbor to replace this former lighthouse.

Cape Poge Light, Chappaquiddick Island.

West Chop Light, Vineyard Haven.

East Chop Light, Oak Bluffs.

145

Edgartown Light, 2008, oil on canvas, 9 x 12.

A New England Fishing Village

Located in the town of Chilmark on the western end of Martha's Vineyard, the small fishing village of Menemsha is a survivor. Battered by hurricanes and pummeled by winter storms over the last century, its name, coming from the Indian language for "still water," seems incongruous to its legacy. Untidy fishermen shacks, jumbled piles of lobster traps and drying nets give the village its particular charm. The compelling aspect of the village is that it looks today as it might have appeared a century ago. At one time, known as Creekville, there was just a narrow inlet leading from Vineyard Sound into Menemsha Pond. In 1905 workers dredged an opening from Menemsha Pond to the sea and by 1910 Menemsha Harbor was a lively, albeit small, fishing port. In 1938 the harbor had to be rebuilt after a devastating hurricane and Dutcher Dock was installed on the east side of the basin. It was named in honor of Rodney Dutcher, a Vineyard native and noted newspaperman. He was 37 years old in 1938 when he died suddenly at his desk in Washington, DC. His reputation was such that President Roosevelt spoke highly of him at a National Press Club affair that same year.

Menemsha Harbor, 2008, oil on canvas, 11 x 14.

Development of Tourism

In 1865 Erastus Carpenter, a wealthy hat manufacturer from Foxboro visited a camp meeting in Wesleyan Grove. At the time, there was a flurry of building activity as permanent cottages were being erected to replace tents. Impressed by the natural beauty of the Vineyard, Carpenter immediately recognized the potential of the island to attract visitors beyond worshipping Methodists. Carpenter, accustomed to fine living, had a vision of large, elegant summer homes, far more elaborate than those in the campgrounds.

The railroad was built in 1874 and the Active (later named the South Beach) operated until 1896 by the Old Colony line. It ran from the Oak Bluffs Wharf to Mattakessett Lodge in Katama. Courtesy www.oldtimeislands.org

Tourism rapidly spread throughout the island to replace the disappearing whaling economy. The Mattakessett Hotel was built as a tourist destination on the outwash plains of Katama in Edgartown. *Courtesy Martha's Vineyard Museum.*

He formed the Oak Bluffs Land and Wharf Company with several other men. The company purchased former grazing land and calling his development "Oak Bluffs," Carpenter successfully sold lots to other well heeled families from Massachusetts and Connecticut. The new development was separated from the camp meeting grounds by Circuit Avenue, named after the route traveling preachers took. After a few mansions were built, Carpenter imagined a way to promote his development. Anticipating large crowds for the 1868 annual camp meeting, he asked new homeowners to decorate their elegant homes with Japanese lanterns. Although those in cottages on the Methodist campground first objected to such an "ungodly" display, they ultimately embraced the custom of "Illumination Night." It remains an Oak Bluff's tradition and is usually held in August.

Ocean Park, Oak Bluffs.

Other growth followed. Architect Samuel F. Pratt of Newport created many impressive structures including the Sea View House which opened in 1872, and Union Chapel. The Flying Horses carousel was built in 1876 as were other hotels. Samuel Winslow, a manufacturer of roller skates from Worcester, Massachusetts built a huge roller skating rink near the Sea View House. Author and historian Arthur G. Railton writes, "More than a thousand buildings were erected in the small area bounded on the east by Vineyard Sound, on the west by the campground, and on the south by Farm Pond." Not like the diminutive campground cottages, they were elaborate and expensive. Vacationers from all over came to the Vineyard.

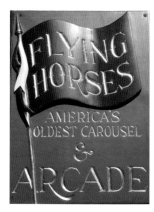

Sign outside the Flying Horses Carousel in Oak Bluffs.

For years, community leaders and townspeople in the cottage city area had been advocating separation from the parent Edgartown. Residents were getting little services for their taxes. Developers and private interests in the camp ground area were the ones who provided water and lighting. Other issues mounted and in 1880, the three developments of Wesleyan Grove, Oak Bluffs resort, and Vineyard Highlands separated and became incorporated as the town of Cottage City. During its glory days, Cottage City was the economic hub of Martha's Vineyard. From open grazing land, it had become one of the most fashionable resorts on the Atlantic seaboard. In 1907, Cottage City was renamed Oak Bluffs.

Unfortunately both the Sea View House and skating rink would be destroyed by fire in 1892. Another fire, which failed to destroy a hotel, was actually started by its owner. Augustus G. Wesley admitted to trying to burn his hotel down for the insurance. After serving three years in jail, he was rehired by the hotel as a cook. The Wesley Hotel, overlooking Lake Avenue still exists. It is the sole survivor of the large hotels prominent in Cottage City's heyday.

The Hotel Wesley in Oak Bluffs has been in continuous operation since 1879.

Cultural Diversity

African-Americans have had a presence on Martha's Vineyard for over three hundred years. However, it wasn't until the post Civil War era in the second half of the 19th century, that their numbers began to increase. Attracted by the island's beauty and the opportunity to work in the growing tourism trade, they came seeking financial security. The post-whaling depression that hit the island made it possible for blacks to afford summer cottages.

African-Americans played a significant role in island politics, helping sway the 1879 vote for the Eastville and Farm Neck areas to secede from Edgartown. In time, a black middle-class community developed as more African-Americans came to enjoy stays in black-owned inns or to purchase summer homes. Almost mythical in its population of elite black educators, attorneys, doctors and celebrities, Oak Bluffs gained a reputation as an elite African-American summer playground. In recent years, as younger generations move away, there has been a decline in the number of black home and business owners. Nevertheless, the black community still maintains a strong sense of place on the Vineyard.

Martha's Vineyard holds special rank as a place where people from different origins have worked together harmoniously since the first colonists came to settle. Relations between whites and native Wampanoags were generally friendly, even during the infamous King Phillip's war in 1675. That conflict, between natives and colonists, spread throughout New England, and although it lasted only a year, resulted in massive fatalities on both sides. Anti-Indian feelings never developed on the Vineyard. In fact, the whaling industry depended on native Wampanoag seamen, as well as those from Africa, Cape Verde, and the Azores who later came to settle.

For those who call the island home, there is a pleasant sense of community. The Black Dog Tavern, an island landmark is an example of islanders coming together in a fun way. The story, as told on the Black Dog website: Prior to 1960 there were no year round eating establishments in town. On a cold evening that year a tired and hungry Captain Robert Douglas, master of the schooner *Shenandoah* had to be content with a cup of bitter coffee and a packaged donut. Deciding to do something about the situation, he sketched out plans for a restaurant on a napkin … actually several napkins, as windows and dormers were considered. He imagined the beach at the head of Vineyard Haven Harbor would be the perfect spot to locate his restaurant, allowing visitors not only a place to eat, but a place to enjoy the harbor and sailing activities outside. The Captain's excitement engaged the attention of other villagers who helped him build and shingle the establishment and who eagerly shared favorite recipes. The name was to honor his favorite canine buddy.

Today, the island with its rich cultural heritage and stunning beauty offers something for everyone. Its mix of small-town New England, elegant resorts, and magnificent shoreline attracts world leaders as well as day trippers. Trendy restaurants abound for every taste and budget. The natural beauty of sea and undisturbed landscape has attracted artists and photographers for over a century. Graceful Victorian era homes, sea captain mansions, and even its famous carousel invite the visitor to learn more about the history of this unique Island. The present is guaranteed to become more meaningful as one explores the past. A good place to start is the Martha's Vineyard Museum on School Street in Edgartown.

Black Dog Tavern, 2008, oil on panel, 9 x 12.

Nantucket Harbor, 2007, oil on canvas, 12 x 16.

CHAPTER ELEVEN
NANTUCKET

We harpooners of Nantucket should be enrolled in the most noble order of St. George. And therefore, let not the knights of that honorable company . . . eye a Nantucketer with disdain, since even in our woolen frocks and tarred trousers we are much better entitled to St. George's decoration than they.
—Herman Melville, *Moby Dick*

Approaching Nantucket by ferry or sailboat, the visitor is greeted by a charming kingdom of shingled cottages nestled closely together underneath the stately golden domed "Old South" church. Sitting high on a bluff among century old trees, the Unitarian Church stands guard over its realm. Once the whaling capital of the world, with hundreds of ships in the harbor, tall masts no longer crowd the view. Barks and schooners have given way to pleasure boats. The last Nantucket vessel in search of the giant sperm whale left in 1869. Long rows of wooden barrels no longer line the wharf. The warehouses and wooden shanties have given up deadeyes and winches for artwork and antiques. Although the maritime industries of Nantucket's yesteryear are no more, there is much that remains to help the visitor relive its vibrant past.

It takes little effort to imagine horse drawn wagons rumbling over cobblestoned town square. Fishing boats, although few in number, help conjure up the comings and goings of scrappy seamen on the docks. The grand columned Atheneum on India Street is as distinctive today as when built in 1847.

Leaving the center of town and walking further up Main Street past the elegant sea captain homes, it's easy to picture a wife penning feelings of loneliness to a husband long at sea. Meandering further along narrow lanes with tiny cottages and ancient backyards, the feeling of antiquity grows even stronger.

It's little wonder that the entire island of Nantucket was designated a National Historic Landmark in 1966.

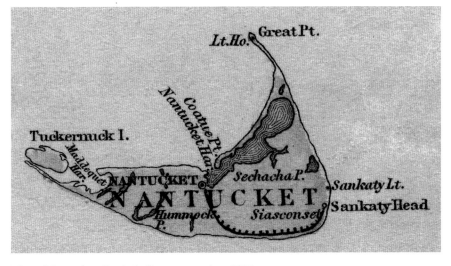

Map of Nantucket. Frank A. Gray, map author, 1881.

Early Settlement

In 1602, when Bartholomew Gosnold first sailed his bark *Concord* past the bluffs of Siasconset on the eastern coast of what we know today as Nantucket, the native Wampanoag tribe were stewards of the land. Their population numbered well over a thousand people. With a land area of 30,000 acres and located 30 miles out to sea, Nantucket was well named. In the native tongue it means "faraway island." A half-century passed after Gosnold put the island on the map before the English actually established a colony there. In 1641 Thomas Mayhew was given the deed to settle Martha's Vineyard, Nantucket, and the Elizabeth Islands. These islands belonged to the jurisdiction of New York until 1692, when they were made a part of Massachusetts.

Mayhew lived on Martha's Vineyard and in 1659, sold 90% of his interest in Nantucket to ten families from Salisbury, Massachusetts. The price was thirty pounds sterling and two beaver hats. The head of one of the families, Thomas Macy, distressed by self-righteous Puritan leaders in his home town, was the first to move to the island with his wife, five children, and three friends. Their dealings with the native Wampanoags were harmonious and this encouraged the remaining nine families to join Macy after a year. The settlers built their homes on the western end of the island in the area of Capaum Pond, close to a small harbor. They named their village Sherburne. Whaling would be years away, but the colonists found ample fishing along the coast. The harbor allowed convenient access for sailing to Martha's Vineyard or the mainland for supplies. In time, shifting sands filled the opening and the settlement moved east toward a larger harbor.

The compact village houses were clustered together with sandy lanes for streets. Although the soil was not particularly rich, corn and other grains were planted. The home of Nathanial and Mary Starbuck was an important focus of island life. The Starbucks converted part of their home into a store and according to historian, A.B.C. Whipple, they sold "everything from 'ribbining' to powder and shot." The Starbucks also sold cider, wine, and rum, "but never to Indians as other settlers did." More significant was the role that Mary played in the community and how it would affect the ultimate character of the town. Born in 1645, Mary was a natural leader. Remarkable in character and mind, she not only was mother to ten children, but was the matriarch of the community. The Starbuck home was a gathering place and important community decisions were made within. Mary's most significant contribution to Nantucket history was her influence converting many of its inhabitants to Quakerism. She had developed a camaraderie with a visiting English Friend, John Richardson, who persuaded her about the merits of Quaker beliefs. After joining that faith when she was fifty-six, and at the height of her influence, she converted many others through her eloquent testimonies. A little over a century later, the Quaker community would grow to almost 2,400 members. They composed the majority of Nantucket whalers and residents for most of the 18th century and strongly influenced architecture, social customs and business practices on the Island.

By many accounts, we are told the white settlers and native Wampanoag tribe lived peacefully. Indeed, Thomas Macy and his family may not have survived that very first winter without the extra food the natives provided. The Indians taught the settlers how to hunt whales and the English, in turn, taught the natives how improve their fishing skills. In the early days of whaling, the native Indians and settlers worked together, enabling them to deploy more boats than the English could have managed alone. The presence of the English colonists nonetheless had a negative impact on the native people. Exposure to disease radically reduced the Indian population. In August 1763, a brig from Ireland cast ashore. One of the crew members, ill with fever, was taken off the vessel and treated in a house frequented by natives. Thought to be either yellow fever or the plague, the disease spread at an alarming rate through the native population. Although the white settlers ministered to the sick as well as they could, the disease was devastating. It killed 222 out of the total 358 natives that lived on the island. Many of those who survived later succumbed to the incapacitating effects of illness and alcohol. Nantucket's last man of part native blood, Abram Quary, died in 1854.

Jethro Coffin House. Built as a wedding gift for Jethro Coffin and Mary Gardner in 1686, it is the only surviving residence from the original English Settlement on Nantucket.

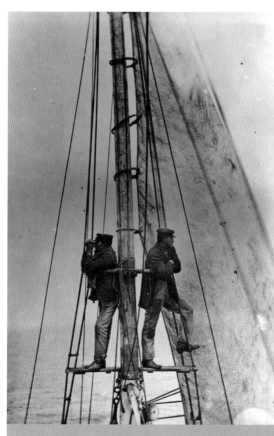

Two crewmen standing in the crow's nest, on lookout for whales aboard a whaling schooner. Unknown date. Courtesy of the Nantucket Historical Association.

Drift Whales on Cliff Bathing Beach, Nantucket. c.1918. Courtesy of the Nantucket Atheneum.

Whaling and the Sea

Long before the great whaling barks and brigantines sailed out of Nantucket Harbor, the Wampanoags knew the value of the drift whales that beached on their shores. They showed the white newcomers how to make use of the harpoon and salvage valuable oil and meat. Later as the numbers of shore whales diminished and it became necessary to seek them in boats, the more experienced Cape Codders were called to help. James Lopar was engaged to come to the island to teach his skills. John Savage, a cooper, was also invited, but it's not known for sure whether these men actually came to Nantucket. In 1690, Ichabod Paddock from Yarmouth accepted the call to help islanders improve their skills killing whales and extracting oil. In time, larger boats were built and men sailed further out to sea in their hunt for the leviathan.

A major boost to the industry came with a chance occurrence. The actual facts are vague, but it's told that during an unexpected winter storm in 1712, a fierce gale blew a Captain Hussey and his crew out to sea in his sloop. They survived, but before returning to land, ran into a school of whales, much larger and with square heads, unlike any they had ever seen. When Captain Hussey brought this prize whale back to Nantucket, there was great excitement over the superior oil it yielded. More importantly, the colonists recognized that the spermaceti, or waxy substance in the head, could be made into high quality candles. Furthermore, a substance called ambergris found in the whale's intestines was even more valued as an ingredient used in perfume manufacturing. Thus began the hunt for the sperm whale. Voyages became longer and crewmen faced increasingly dangerous challenges.

When a whale was sighted, seamen took pursuit in smaller open whale-boats. The mother ship usually carried three or more harpooners. Skilled and strong, they ranked higher than other seamen. Instead of having to sleep in the cramped forecastle of the ship, they had better sleeping and eating conditions. The harpoon, when thrown, was attached to hundreds of feet of line. When the harpooner successfully speared a victim, the whale would bolt up and speed away dragging the boat on a "Nantucket sleigh ride." It usually took hours for the whale to tire at which point the men finished it off with lances and hauled it back to the mother ship. The whale was chained alongside the vessel and crew members lowered a platform to begin "cutting in." Long strips of blubber were removed, hauled on board and cut up into smaller chunks. The blubber would be put into large kettles and boiled to remove the oil, a process known as "trying." In the early days of whaling, the carcasses would have to be brought back to shore for processing. Later, stoves and tryworks for boiling the blubber were installed on ships eliminating the need to return for this operation.

In 1723 Richard Macy built Nantucket's first town wharf, known today as Straight Wharf. Warehouses were built as were shops for blacksmiths, coopers, and sail makers. The population of the town increased in number and wealth. Trade expanded further in 1745 when the first island vessel sailed to England to sell its cargo of whale oil. By sailing directly and avoiding the Boston middle-men, merchants made higher profits. In addition, goods such as iron, sailcloth, and hardware items could be purchased at cheaper prices abroad and brought home. The vessels at this time were generally sloops of sixty to seventy tons.

Earliest photographic view of Straight Wharf. c.1890s. *Courtesy of the Nantucket Historical Association.*

Men on whaleboat in harbor "cutting in" dead whale alongside boat. c.1860s. *Courtesy of the Nantucket Historical Association.*

On January 24, 1746 at a town meeting in the village of Sherburne, as Nantucket was then known, the sea captains of the island appealed for a lighthouse to better guide them into port. Two hundred English pounds were appropriated to build the light, but only on the condition that the ship captains maintain it. This first lighthouse, a primitive wooden structure, lasted for only 12 years when a fire, possibly started by spilled lamp oil that ignited, destroyed the structure in 1758. Approved at town meeting, a new light house was built the next year. It stood only 15 years until 1774. A news report in the *Massachusetts Gazette and the Boston Post-Boy and Advertiser* stated:

> *We hear from Nantucket that on Wednesday the 9th of March (1774) at about 8 o'clock in the morning, they had a most violent gust of wind that perhaps was ever known there, but it lasted only about a minute. It seemed to come in a narrow vein, and in its progress blew down and totally destroyed the light-house on that island, besides several shops, barns, etc."*

Storms and fire continued to play havoc with the building and it would be rebuilt six additional times. In 1901, the tenth light and seventh tower were built at the extremity of the point. The white cylindrical (wooden) tower still exists with a footbridge to shore. Now part of the Coast Guard installation on Brant Point, the light station, only 26 feet in height, is the lowest lighthouse in New England. It has a red light eclipsed every four seconds.

Brant Point Light, 2007, oil on panel, 8 x 10.

Two other lighthouses on Nantucket cast a welcoming beacon to mariners. Sankaty Head Light, recently moved inland from its hazardous position on the edge of Sankaty bluff, was first lit in 1850. Cliff erosion threatened toppling the tower into the ocean 100 feet below. It was the first U.S. lighthouse to receive a Fresnel lens as part of its original equipment. Mariners, seeing its light 20 miles at sea, affectionately called it the "blazing star." Its red stripe still serves as a day marker. Sankaty Light has a flashing white light every 7.5 seconds.

Great Point Light, originally built in 1785, has had several lives. Destroyed by fire in 1816, a new 60-foot tower was built in 1818. Cliff erosion threatened the tower and ultimately a spring storm in 1984 wrecked havoc, reducing it to a pile of rubble. Two years later, a replica 300 yards west of the old tower was erected. At its relighting ceremony, U.S. Senator Edward Kennedy proudly exclaimed, "Great Point is alive and well again." It has a flashing white light every five seconds.

Sankaty Head Light overlooks the eastern shore of Nantucket. *Courtesy www.rudyalicelighthouse.net.*

Great Point Light is on the northeast corner of Nantucket. First lit in 1986, the foundation on the new tower was placed 35 feet below ground. It has a modern optic powered by solar panels.

Effects of Wars

There were over one hundred and fifty vessels in the Nantucket whaling fleet in 1775. Almost every young man on the island was involved in a trade connected to the industry: carpenter, rope-maker, cooper or blacksmith. When the Revolutionary War broke out, it was devastating to the island. Most of the residents were forced into a state of inactivity making subsistence extremely difficult. Since many Nantucketers were pacifist Quakers and many others were Loyalists, they attempted to remain neutral. In doing so they became enemies to both sides and were cut off from the world. The presence of British war ships and privateers brought the whaling industry to an abrupt halt. It's been estimated that over one hundred ships with cargo and crew were captured or sunk by the British. The drastic winter of 1780 further exacerbated the suffering. Between the war, hunger, and exposure to cold, it's estimated that over sixteen hundred people died. The schooners and square riggers tied up in the harbor deteriorated and became useless.

After the war recovery was slow, but advances were gradually made. A breakthrough came in 1791 when Captain Paul Worth sailed his ship *Beaver* around Cape Horn. Until then, sailors had great trepidation sailing this stretch of treacherous water between South America and Antarctica. The area is plagued by gale-force winds, massive waves and icebergs. But when Captain Worth brought home his extremely profitable hoard of oil he opened the way for a new whale hunting ground. Meanwhile in 1795, the

earlier village name of Sherburne was officially changed to Nantucket. Ship-related trades flourished as did candle making. Quaker businessman, William Rotch built the first candle factory at the head of Straight Wharf in 1770. By 1792, there were ten candle works on the island. A decade later there were nineteen. The reborn prosperity in whaling and associated trades was cut short by the War of 1812. For a second time, the town and vessels were at the mercy of the British fleet. By declaring neutrality, they could fish offshore for cod or obtain the firewood needed for heating. But once again, even though the war only lasted two years, the whaling fleet suffered. By the end of the war there were only twenty-three vessels left.

View Across Nantucket Harbor with Unitarian Universalist Church in the distance and fishing fleet in the foreground. c.1900. *Courtesy of the Nantucket Atheneum.*

A Captain's Life at Sea

Undaunted, the industrious Quakers began rebuilding ships and were once again bringing home their valuable payload of oil. When the rich whaling grounds off Chile, Peru, and then Japan were discovered in 1819 it opened the way to riches never imagined. Between 1820 and 1830 Nantucket had 237 ships in service and was indisputably the whaling capital of the world. The largest hunting area was in the Pacific Ocean where sperm whales were the most plentiful. In contrast to the romanticized picture that many have about a captain's life at sea, the trips took every ounce of courage and stamina humanly possible. Captain Samuel Joy (1795-1843) began his career at sea as a ten-year old crew member on the whaling ship *Atlas* under the command of his father, Reuben Joy. When Samuel was 22, he served as second mate on the *Essex*, the ill-fated ship that would in later years be immortalized in "Moby Dick." His journal entries from a whaling voyage he commanded on the ship *Mary Mitchell* from 1835 to 1838 give an intimate look at the trials, frustrations, and disappointments a whaling shipmaster faced. Just three weeks into his journey off the coast of West Africa, Captain Joy wrote (original spelling and punctuation):

Saw finbacks but nothing else the ground is terrible barren and I am fairly tired and, I expected to have had 300 bbls. Now by others talk of this ground I am however disappointed no unusual thing for me my life had been a tissue of disappointment the Will o the Lord be done.

Seeing no prey, Captain Joy took the *Mary Mitchell* around the Cape of Good Hope. Although he had somewhat better luck and took four whales several weeks later, he recorded:

Nantucket Whaling Ship. *Courtesy of the Nantucket Atheneum.*

*Heavy gales and hard squalls with a tremendous sea cut up our blubber put it
into casks and got some oil between decks ship labors hard and the scene above and
around us beggars all description let no man ever talk to me again about whaling in
this country.*

In addition to the main objective of finding whales, a captain's responsibilities were
enormous. Author, Leslie W. Ottinger, writes,

*There was supervising and directing the crew in maintaining, repairing, and sailing the
ship. And there was the critical issue of navigation, often with charts that were not entirely
accurate. His central task was to find whales; and when he did, he was responsible for
directing those who killed them, brought them to the ship, cut them in, ran the tryworks,
and stowed the oil. A whale ship was self-sustaining, and the captain had to find ways to
replenish the supplies of food, water, and wood as they went along. He had to recruit new
men, since desertion was common.*

Certainly not the least of his duties, the captain also had to serve as ship physician
and deal with frequent injuries, broken limbs, and diseases such as dysentery and scurvy. A
journal entry from Captain Joy reveals his lack of confidence in this area. After ministering
to seaman David Mitchell he wrote: "I am afraid all is not as it ought to be I pray we may
fall in with some ship having a surgeon." Captain Joy was relieved when the surgeon from
a passing bark pronounced the patient's bones "well set." After a thirty-four month voyage,
harvesting the oil from fifty-seven whales, Captain Joy and his crew returned. He did not go
to sea again and died five years later at the age of forty-seven.

Captain Charles Grant. *Courtesy of the Nantucket Atheneum.*

Equal to a sea captain's physical challenge was the emotional strain of being away from home and family. Elizabeth Shore, in her article "Whalers' Letters," tells of Captain Charles E. Alien, on board the bark *Sea Ranger*. He wrote the following letter to his daughter on Sunday, November 5, 1871.

Dear daughter Emma, as I have been sitting here in my cabin, alone and lonely, the thought rushed into my mind: Is this all of life? My heart answered no. This is part which goes to make up the grand whole. In truth I should feel very Sad if there was nothing more comforting for me than the knowledge that this whaling voyage commenced Oct. 9th 1869 and after passing through its various changes of ill success and good success, of Storm and Tempest, of trials by man, by Leviathan, and the Elements, I must, if spared return to my home at Nantucket, Four years farther on toward the end of my Pilgrimage, worn down in body, unfit for labor at home, and temporally poorer than when I embarked: but I have a hope that all this is not to be and that the End will produce a brighter and newer beautiful picture.

Life was equally lonely for the wives and family members left behind. Phebe Folger Coleman wrote the following to her husband, Captain Samuel Coleman who was at sea.

Nantucket 9th mo. 19th 1808
Dear Husband,
I have felt a little guilty that I have deferred so long to write: but I had nothing worth communicating, nothing but what thou might reasonably suppose, that is, that I am very lonesome. Why should so much of our time be spent apart, why do we refuse the happiness that is within our reach? Is the acquisition of wealth an adequate compensation for the tedious hours of absence? To me it is not. The enjoyment of riches alone could give no satisfaction to me. In company I am not happy, I feel as if a part of myself was gone. Thy absence grows more insupportable than it used to be. I want for nothing but thy company: but there is nothing but what I could do better without....

Captain Charles Grant is considered by many to be Nantucket's most famous whaling master. In *One Hundred Years on Nantucket* he is described as having "brought into port more oil than any other captain in the history of the world's whale fishery and made more money than any man who ever speared a whale." In 1825, when he first went to sea, he was boy of eleven. He was master of the ship *Walter Scott* when he was thirty and the voyage netted over $100,000. He would command many other ships, among them the *Potomac*, the *Mohawk*, the *Milton*, and the *Horatio*. His voyage in the *Milton* was the most profitable, netting $190,000. His share was $25,000. During his career at sea he brought in 52,000 barrels of sperm oil, 12,000 pounds of whalebone and 18 pounds of ambergris.

Island Life

During the golden years of whaling, Nantucket was a bustling town. The candle factories, cooperages, and rope shops thrived. Any craftsman with a skill related to sailing had plenty to do. As Quakerism waned, Nantucket became a very wealthy and fashionable island city. Triumphant whaling captains built elegant mansions in Georgian or neo-Greek tradition. Although almost all Nantucket whaling boats were built in other areas of Massachusetts or Connecticut, a modest shipyard turned out small boats. Warehouses were filled with spices or imported goods from exotic places. There were four banks and three newspapers. Women far outnumbered men. In addition to the widows and spinsters, many married women had to exist for years at a time while their husbands were at sea. The usual length of a whaling trip was three to five years. Being on their own, most women developed good management skills and resourcefulness. In addition to running homes and raising children, they handled financial matters and many started small home businesses. *Petticoat Row* on Centre Street, later destroyed in the Great Fire, was named after the women merchants who sold sundries and imported goods. Women were generally the ones who ministered to the sick, often using medicinal herbs and techniques earlier learned from the native Wampanoags.

The Three Bricks. Nos. 93, 95, 97 Main Street, Nantucket. These identical redbrick homes, with columned Greek-revival porches at their front entrances, were built between 1836 and 1838 by whaling merchant Joseph Starbuck for his three sons.

Greek Revival Mansions at 94 and 96 Main Street, Nantucket.

The "old-time" scene on South Wharf presented a much different picture than today's flower-decked galleries. It was home to the majority of scallop shanties on Nantucket. These were the places where scallopers brought their harvest to be treated by "openers." Edouard A. Stackpole described a typical shanty scene in *Once Along the Waterfront*:

… the small stove mounted high in the center of the room; the variety of oil lamps throwing a glow of yellow light over all, bringing out the dark shadows cast by the gear stowed away overhead; the "openers" hunched on stools over the benches piled high with scallops; the smell of pipe-smoke and chewing tobacco, and, most important of all, the voices of the men themselves — most of whom have long since departed. No more colorful an experience than to be among the most youthful of those who participated.

Old South Wharf, 2007, oil on panel, 9 x 12.

Hard Times for the Island

Several successive events caused a dramatic downturn in Nantucket's fortunes and economy. As whaling voyages became longer and larger ships were required, the harbor became inadequate. Nantucket would ultimately surrender its preeminence as the whaling capital of the world to New Bedford, Massachusetts. In 1846 there were sixteen whaling ships registered in Nantucket compared to sixty-nine in New Bedford. The whaling industry and economy of the town was further severely damaged by four successive events. No one knows exactly how it started, but what became known as "The Great Fire" broke out about 11 p.m. on July 13, 1846, in the hat store of William H. Geary on Main Street. In his *History of Nantucket, 2nd edition*, Obed Macy quotes one of the first witnesses after the alarm was sounded, "a good smart stream of water at this juncture, would have quenched the flames, which were in a few moments bursting from the roof."

Sadly, there was no water at hand and the fire spread, raging through the wharves and downtown, fueled by long rows of oil barrels. The damage was catastrophic and included the Athenaeum library and its collections, two newspapers, seven oil factories, the Episcopal Church and over 300 buildings including most of the business section of town. As testament to the positive spirit and energy of the townspeople, sixty stores and shops were well along in reconstruction at the end of six weeks. Although the burned area was rebuilt, many business owners never fully recovered from the fire.

The second blow was the California Gold Rush in 1849. Young men that might have gone to sea on whaling ships made their way out west. Nantucket lost a quarter of its men to the gold fields. Ten years later, an oil well erected by Edwin Drake in Titusville, Pennsylvania, successfully yielded ground oil. Refining methods were quickly developed and whale oil became history. The final

Young man looking at the town of Nantucket from a field. c.1900. *Courtesy of the Nantucket Atheneum.*

event that put Nantucket economy on a downward spiral was the Civil War. The island remained in a severe economic depression for almost a century. Many left to seek work and establish homes elsewhere. Between 1840 and 1870, census figures show a loss of 60 percent of the island's population. The bright side is that this long lasting downturn resulted in the island retaining its unique authentic character. No industries came in, nor would development change the town's historic complexion.

Siasconset Village with *Auld Lang Syne* on left, 1905. *Courtesy of the Nantucket Atheneum.*

Tourism Develops

Before off-islanders discovered the little haven of Siasconset on the eastern end of Nantucket, wealthier villagers would go there during the summer months. S'conset, as it's called by the locals, sits on a bluff on the southeastern tip of the island overlooking ocean and moors. Originally its diminutive cottages were shabby fishermen huts. First settled in the 17th century and known as "Codfish Park," it was a humble colony of unadorned shingle-sided shanties with crude board chimneys and rough and untidy accommodations. During their "off-season" in the middle of stifling July days, fishermen would rent their shacks to more affluent Nantucketers who craved cooling ocean breezes.

Importantly, it was a place to escape the fetid odor of boiling whale oil that enveloped the main part of town. Although it attracted affluent islanders, it was not a place of fashionable living. Describing the cottages A. Judd Northrup wrote: "A S'conset cottage parlor is a small affair, but it will very likely hold all your friends—provided you take several evenings for it and entertain them in sections." By 1880 the American tradition of summer vacations was becoming established. Nantucket, with its extensive beaches, saltwater bathing and refreshing sea breezes, offered an idyllic spot to visit. Hotels were built in town as well as in outlying areas such as Surfside and Siasconset.

S'conset Cottages, 2007, oil on canvas panel, 9 x 12.

Auld Lang Syne, 2007, oil on canvas, 9 x 12.

At the beginning of the 20th century, a three-man Committee on Advertising created a flyer titled, *Nantucket Island: An Ideal Health and Vacation Resort*. Several decades later in 1934 the Nantucket Island Chamber of Commerce was founded and sought to preserve the traditions and promote the prosperity of the island.

Surf Bathing on S'conset Beach. c.1918. *Courtesy of the Nantucket Atheneum.*

Nantucket View, 2007,
watercolor on paper, 14 x 18.

The Nantucket landscape has diverse and stunning characteristics that set it apart aesthetically from the rest of America. The scenery is ever-changing depending on the season. There are over 80 miles of pristine beaches, open rolling grasslands or "moors," kettle ponds, wetlands and one of the largest natural cranberry bogs in the world. Owned by the Nantucket Conservation Foundation, the bog is over 260 acres in size. More than 35% of island land has been protected through the work of public and private conservation groups. This conservation land is open to the public for walking and birding and will always be preserved. Heath, ivy and wild roses, imported from Scotland, England and Japan respectively, grow in abundance. Hydrangea bushes seem to border every cottage. Deer, ring-necked pheasant, rabbits and geese are plentiful. Prolific numbers of migrating birds fly overhead.

The cottages at the Boat Basin provide a popular way to experience Nantucket. Just a short walk from historic downtown, sightseers enjoy a unique experience. Galleries and shops are filled with the work of local artisans. Restaurants accommodate every taste from take-out to world-class dining. The impressive Whaling Museum on nearby Broad Street, transports the visitor back through Nantucket's glorious past. Although many things have changed and the majestic whaling ships have been replaced by pleasure boats, the sea and sky and legacy of Nantucket are as brilliant as ever.

Nantucket Getaway, 2007, oil on canvas, 9 x 12.

RESOURCES

Art Organizations on Cape Cod and the Islands.

Cape Cod Museum of Art
Route 6A
Dennis, MA 02638
Phone (508) 385-4477
www.ccmoa.org

Cape Cod Art Association
3480 Route 6A
Barnstable, MA 02630
Phone: (508) 362-2909
www.capecodartassoc.org

Provincetown Art Association and Museum
460 Commercial Street
Provincetown, MA 02657
Phone: (508) 487-1750
www.paam.org

Cahoon Museum of American Art
4676 Falmouth Road
Cotuit, MA 02635
Phone: (508) 428-7581
www.cahoonmuseum.org

Fine Arts Work Center in Provincetown
24 Pearl Street
Provincetown, MA 02657
Phone: (508) 487-9960
www.fawc.org

Falmouth Artists Guild
311 Rear Main Street
Falmouth, MA 02540
Phone: (508) 540-3304
www.falmouthart.org

For more information about the arts on Cape Cod contact:

Arts Foundation of Cape Cod
3 Shoot Flying Hill Rd.
Centerville, MA 02632
Phone: (508)362-0066
www.artsfoundation.org

Artists Association of Nantucket
PO Box 1104
Nantucket, MA 02554
Phone: (508) 228-0722
www.nantucketarts.org

Martha's Vineyard Art Association
Old Sculpin Gallery
Dock Street
Edgartown, MA 02539
Phone: (508) 627-4881
www.oldsculpingallery.org

For a complete listing of Massachusetts Art Museums, Non-profit Art Organizations and Art Centers please go to:
www.art-collecting.com/nonprofits_ma

Historical Societies and Museums on Cape Cod and the Islands

Please note: Many of the following organizations are open on a seasonal basis. It's advisable to call for hours of operation before planning a visit.

Aptucxet Trading Post Museum
24 Aptucxet Road
Bourne, MA 02532
Phone: (508) 759-8167 or (508) 759-9487
www.bournehistoricalsoc.org

Barnstable Historical Society
3074 Main Street
Route 6A, Old Kings Highway
Barnstable, MA 02630
Phone: (508) 362-2982
www.sturgislibrary.org

Bourne Historical Society
30 Keene Street
PO Box 3095
Bourne, MA 02532-0795
Phone: (508) 759-8167
www.bournehistoricalsoc.org

Brewster Historical Society and Museum
Box 1146
Brewster, MA 02631
Phone: (508) 896-9521
www.brewsterhistoricalsociety.org

Cape Cod Maritime Museum
135 South Street
Hyannis, MA 02601
Phone: (508) 775-1706
www.capecodmaritimemuseum.org

Cape Cod Museum of Natural History
869 Main Street, Route 6A
Brewster, MA 02631
Phone: (508) 896-3867
www.ccmnh.org

Centerville Historical Society and Museum
513 Main Street
Centerville, MA 02632
Phone: (508) 775-0331
www.centervillehistoricalmuseum.org

Chatham Historical Society & Atwood House Museum
347 Stage Harbor Road
Chatham, MA 02633
Phone: (508) 945-2493
www.chathamhistoricalsociety.org

Cotuit Museum of American Art
4676 Route 28
Cotuit, MA 02635
Phone (508) 428-7581
www.cahoonmuseum.org

Coast Guard Heritage Museum
3353 Main Street, Route 6A
Barnstable Village, MA 02630
Phone: (508) 362-8521
www.coastguardheritagemuseum.org

Dennis Historical Society
PO Box 607
South Dennis, MA 02660
Phone: (508) 385-2232
www.dennishistsoc.org

Dexter Grist Mill
Town Square
Sandwich, MA 02563
Phone: (508) 888-5144

Eastham Historical Society & Schoolhouse Museum
PO Box 8
Eastham, MA 02642
Phone: (508) 240-8071
www.easthamhistorical.org

Eastham Windmill
Route 6A and Samoset Road
Eastham, MA 02642
Phone: (508) 240-5900

Falmouth Historical Society & Museums on the Green
55 Palmer Avenue
Falmouth, MA 02540
Phone: (508) 548-4857
www.falmouthhistoricalsociety.org

Green Briar Nature Center
6 Discovery Hill Road
East Sandwich, MA 02537
Phone: (508) 888-6870
www.thorntonburgess.org

Harwich Historical Society and Brooks Academy
Museum
80 Parallel Street
Harwich, MA 02645
Phone: (508) 432-8089
www.harwichhistoricalsociety.org

Historical Society of Old Yarmouth
11 Strawberry Lane
Yarmouth Port, MA 02675
Phone: (508) 362-5017
www.hsoy.org

Historical Society of Santuit and Cotuit
1148 Main Street
Cotuit, MA 02635
Phone: (508) 428-0461
www.cotuithistoricalsociety.org

Hoxie House
18 Water Street
Sandwich, MA 02563
Phone: (508) 888-1173

Martha's Vineyard Museum/Historical Society
59 School Street
Edgartown, MA 02539
Phone: (508) 627-4441
www.mvmuseum.org

Nantucket Atheneum
1 India Street
Nantucket, MA 02554
Phone (508) 228-1110
www.nantucketatheneum.org

Nantucket Historical Association and Whaling
Museum
15 Broad Street
Nantucket, MA 02554
Phone: (508) 228-5785
www.nha.org

National Sea Shore Salt Pond Visitor Center
Off Route 6A
Eastham, MA 02653
Phone: (508) 255-3421
www.nps.gov/caco

New England Fire and History Museum
1439 Main Street, Route 6A
Brewster, MA 02631
Phone: (508) 896-5711

Orleans Historical Society
3 River Road
Orleans, MA 02653
Phone: (508) 240-1329
www.orleanshistoricalsoceity.org

Osterville Historical Society
155 West Bay Road
Osterville, MA 02655
Phone: (508) 428-5861
www.ostervillage.com/Osterville-Historical-Society

Pilgrim Monument and Provincetown Museum
One High Pole Hill Road
Provincetown, MA 02657
Phone: (508) 487-1310
www.pilgrim-monument.org

Provincelands Visitor Center
Race Point Road – Off Route 6A
Provincetown, MA 02657
Phone: (508) 487-1256 (summer) or
(508) 487-2123 (winter)

Sandwich Glass Museum/Sandwich Historical Society
129 Main Street
PO Box 103
Sandwich, MA 02563
Phone (508) 888-0251
www.sandwichglassmuseum.org

Tales of Cape Cod, Inc.
Old Colonial Courthouse
Barnstable Village, MA
www.talesofcapecod.org

Thornton Burgess Museum
4 Water Street
PO Box 972
Sandwich, MA 02563
Phone: (508)888-4668 or (508)888-6870
www.thorntonburgess.org

Truro Historical Society/Highland Light Museum
27 Highland Road
N. Truro, MA 02666
Phone: (508) 487-3397
www.trurohistorical.org

Wellfleet Historical Society
266 Main Street
Wellfleet, MA 02667
Phone: (508) 349-9157
www.wellfleethistoricalsociety.com

William Brewster Nickerson Cape Cod History Archives
Cape Cod Community College
2240 Iyannough Road
West Barnstable, MA 02668-1599
Phone: (508) 362-2131
www.capecod.edu/web/library/nickerson

Woods Hole Historical Museum
573 Woods Hole Road
PO Box 185
Woods Hole, MA 02543
Phone: (508) 548-7270
www.woodsholemuseum.org

BIBLIOGRAPHY

Archer, Gabriel. *Bartholomew Gosnold's Discovery of Cape Cod. 2002.* The Legacy Preservation Library. www.usgennet.org/topic/preservation/epochs/vol 2/pg38 (accessed July 10, 2008).

Banks, Charles Edward, MD. *The History of Martha's Vineyard, Dukes County, Massachusetts.* Volume 1. Edgartown, MA: Dukes County Historical Society, 1966.

Barber, John Warner. *Historical collections being a general collection of interesting facts, traditions, biographical sketches, anecdotes, &c., relating to the history and antiquities of every town in Massachusetts with geographical descriptions.* Worcester, MA: Dorr, Howland & Co., 1839.

Beston, Henry. *The Outermost House: A Year of Life on the Great Beach of Cape Cod.* New York, NY: Doubleday, 1928.

Black Dog Tavern website: www.theblackdog.com (accessed September 12, 2008).

Bradford, William. *History of Plymouth Plantation: 1620-1647.* Boston, MA: The Massachusetts Historical Society, 1912.

Brigham, Albert Perry. *Cape Cod and the Old Colony.* New York and London: G.P. Putnam's Sons, 1920.

Burgess, Thornton W. *Now I Remember: Autobiography of an amateur naturalist.* Boston, MA: Little Brown, 1960.

Cahill, Robert Ellis. *Olde New England's Sugar and Spice and Everything.* Salem, MA: Old Saltbox Publishing House, Inc., 1991.

Cape Cod and All the Pilgrim Land. June 1922, Volume 6, Number 4. A Monthly Magazine Devoted to the Interests of Southeastern Massachusetts. Project Gutenburg, www.gutenberg.org/etext/14979 (accessed July 13, 2008).

Cappelloni, Nancy. *Cranberry Cooking For All Season.* New Bedford, MA: Spinner Publications, Inc., 2002.

Carson, Rachel. *Under the Sea Wind.* New York, NY: Penguin Books, 1941.

Claflin, James. *Lighthouses and Life Saving Along the Massachusetts Coast.* Charleston, SC: Arcadia, 1998.

Corbett, Scott. *Cape Cod's Way.* New York, NY: Thomas Y. Crowell Company, 1955.

Cranberries on Cape Cod. Hartford, CT: *Hartford Times*, Sept 28, 1891.

Daley, Beth. *The Shifting Sands of Cape Cod. The Boston Globe.* December 17, 2006.

Deyo, Simeon L., editor. *History of Barnstable County, Massachusetts.* New York, NY: H.W. Blake & Co., 1890.

Dolphin, Debbie. *Gay Head Light: Aquinnah Light Station.* June 15, 2007. www.home.comcast.net/~debee2/mass/GayHead (accessed May 16, 2008).

Drake, Samuel Adams. *Nooks and Corners of the New England Coast.* New York, NY: Harper & Brothers, 1875.

Edwards, Agnes. *Cape Cod New and Old.* Boston, MA and New York, NY: Houghton Mifflin Co., 1918.

Falmouth Chamber of Commerce. *Fact Sheet, Falmouth Massachusetts.* Dec.27, 2005. www.falmouthchamber.com (accessed July 10, 2008).

Farson, Robert H. *The Cape Cod Canal.* Yarmouth Port, MA: Cape Cod Historical Publications, 1977.

Farson, Robert H. *Cape Cod Railroads.* Yarmouth Port, MA: Cape Cod Historical Publications, 1993.

Fawsett, Marise. *Cape Cod Annals.* Bowie, MA: Heritage Books, Inc., 1990.

Fawsett, Marise. *Sandwich, The Oldest Town on Cape Cod.* East Sandwich, MA: Published by the author, 1969.

Finch, Robert. *Cape Cod: Its Natural and Cultural History; A Guide to Cape Cod National Seashore, Massachusetts.* Produced by the Division of Publications, National Park Service, U.S. Department of the Interior, 1993.

Fiore, Jordan D, Editor. *Mourt's Relation: A Journal of the Pilgrims of Plymouth.* Plymouth, MA: Plymouth Rock Foundation, 1985.

Ford Tricia, compiler. *First Encounter with a Turnip.* Eastham MA: Friends of the Eastham Public Library, 2007.

Halter, Marilyn. *Between Race and Ethnicity: Cape Verdean American Immigrants, 1860-1965.* Urbana, IL: University of Illinois Press, c1993.

Handy, Amy L., editor. *What We Cook on Cape Cod.* Hyannis, MA: F.B. & F.P. Goss, 1911.

Historical Society of Old Yarmouth. *Overview of Yarmouth History: Native Americans.* 2004. www.hsoy.org/history (accessed June 20, 2008).

Kaye, Glen. *Cape Cod: The Story Behind the Scenery*. Las Vegas, NV: KC Publications, Inc., 1980.

Kern, Florence. *Letters from Two Attics Provide More Insight on Capt. Wm. Pease*. The Dukes County Intelligencer, Vol.28, No.1 August, 1986.

Kerr, John. *Salt Marshes Were Early Valued Sources of Hay*. Cape Cod Summer Times. Hyannis, MA. July 8, 1972.

Kittredge, Henry C. *Cape Cod Its People and Their History*. Hyannis, MA: Parnassus Imprints, Inc., 1987.

Kittredge, Henry C. *Shipmasters of Cape Cod*. Hyannis, MA: Parnassus Imprints, Inc., 1998.

Lane, Ferdinand C. *On Old Cape Cod*. Orleans, MA: Cape Codder Printery, 1961.

Lawrence, Mary Chipman. *The Captain's Best Mate: the journal of Mary Chipman Lawrence on the whaler Addison, 1856-1860*. Providence, RI: Brown University Press, 1966.

Lillie, Frank Rattray. *The Woods Hole Marine Biological Laboratory*. Chicago, IL: University of Chicago Press, 1944.

Lovell, R.A. Jr. *Sandwich, A Cape Cod Town*. Sandwich, MA: Published by the Town of Sandwich, 1996.

Massachusetts. Department of Labor and Industries. *Population and Resources of Cape Cod. A Special Report in Recognition of the Three Hundredth Anniversary of the Settlement of New England*. Boston, MA: Wright & Potter Printing Company, State Printers, 1922.

Megan, Kate. *I Play in the Secret Pond*. 1998. Public Domain www.jade-leaves.com/journal/misc/pond_poems (accessed Aug. 14, 2008).

Newcomb, Steve. *Five Hundred Years of Injustice*. Shaman's Drum. Fall 1992. www.ili.nativeweb.org/sdrm_art (accessed August 5, 2008).

Northrup, A. Judd. *Sconset Cottage Life: A Summer on Nantucket Island*. Syracuse, NY: C.W. Bardeen, 1881.

Norton, Henry Franklin. *Martha's Vineyard: Historical, Legendary, Scenic: the Story of its Towns, Edgartown, Oak Bluffs, Tisbury (Vineyard Haven), West Tisbury, Chilmark, Gay Head*. Hartford, CN: The Author, 1923.

O'Brien, Greg, editor. *A Guide to Nature on Cape Cod and the Islands*. Hyannis, MA: Parnassus Imprints, 1995.

O'Connell, James C. *Becoming Cape Cod*. Hanover, NH: University Press of New England, 2003.

Otis, Amos. *Genealogical Notes of Barnstable Families*. Barnstable, MA: F. B. & F. P. Goss, 1888.

Ottinger, Leslie W. *Good Bye Mary Mitchell Hard Lucky Craft: Captain Samuel Joy's Journal, 1835-38*. Nantucket Historical Association online article. nd. http://www.nha.org/history/hn/HNcaptjoy (accessed September 15, 2008).

Parkman, Francis et al. *History of the Humane Society of Massachusetts*. Boston, MA: Samuel N. Dickinson Printer. 1845.

Peters, Russell M. *The Wampanoags of Mashpee: an Indian Perspective on American History*. Jamaica Plain, MA: R.M. Peters, 1987.

Quinn, William P. *The Saltworks of Historic Cape Cod*. Orleans, MA: Parnassus Imprints, 1993.

Railton, Arthur, R. *The History of Martha's Vineyard*. Beverly, MA: Commonwealth Editions, 2006.

Roberts, Callum. *The Unnatural History of the Sea*. New York: Harper Collins, 2007.

Russell, Howard S. *A Long, Deep Furrow: Three Centuries of Farming in New England*. Hanover, NH: University Press of New England, 1976.

Schneider, Paul. *The Enduring Shore*. New York, NY: Henry Holt and Company, 2000.

Schuler, Stanley. *The Cape Cod House*. Exton, PA: Schiffer Publishing Ltd., 1982.

Sears, J. Henry. *Brewster Ship Masters*. Yarmouth Port, MA: C.W. Swift Publisher, 1906.

Stackpole, Edouard A. *Once Along the Waterfront*. Historic Nantucket, Vol. 43, no. 2 (Summer 1994).

Shore, Elizabeth. "Whaler's Letters." *Historic Nantucket*, Vol 44, no 2 (Fall 1995), pp. 90-92.

Starbuck, Alexander. *The History of Nantucket*. Boston, MA: C.E. Goodspeed & CO.,1924.

Strother, D.H. *Summer in New England, Second Paper*. Harper's New Monthly Magazine. Sept 1860. Volume 21, Issue 124, pp. 442-461.

Thoreau, Henry David. *Cape Cod*. New York, NY: Penquin Books. 1987

Town of Chatham Massachusetts. *About Chatham*. n.d. www.town.chatham.ma.us/Public Documents/ChathamMA_WebDocs/about (accessed July 11, 2008).

Wellfleet Local Planning Committee. *Setting a Course for our Future: the 1995 local comprehensive plan*. Wellfleet, MA: Wellfleet Local Planning Committee. 1995.

U.S. Coast Guard. *Brant Point Light*. Historic Light Station Information & Photography. 1998. www.uscg.mil/history/WEBLIGHTHOUSES/LHMA (accessed Aug. 23, 2008).

U.S. Highbush Blueberry Council. *The Highbush Blueberry History*. 2002. www.blueberry.org/blueberries (accessed July 20, 2008)

Wampanoag Tribe of Gay Head (Aquinnah). n.d. www.wampanoagtribe.net/Pages/Wampanoag_WebDocs/history_culture (accessed May 16, 2008).

Waldron, Les. *Personal Communication*. July 12, 2006.

Waldron, Nan Turner. *Journey to the Outermost House*. Bethlehem, CN: Butterfly and Wheel Publishing. 1991.

Webster, Fletcher, ed. *The Private Correspondence of Daniel Webster*. Boston, MA: Little Brown and Company. 1857.

Whipple, A.B.C. *Vintage Nantucket*. New York: Dodd, Mead, c1978.

Wellfleet Chamber of Commerce. Wellfleet History. n.d. www.wellfleetchamber.com/History July 1, 2008.

Whittier, John Greenleaf. *The Complete Poetical Works of John Greenleaf Whittier*. Boston, MA: James R. Osgood and Company. 1873.

Winslow, Edward. *How the Pilgrims Lived*. National Center for Public Policy Research. www.nationalcenter.org/Pilgrims (accessed August 5, 2008)

Zuniga, Britt Steen. *Images of America: Centerville*. Charleston, SC: Arcadia, c.2001.